CW00924687

Marsden

A Journey Through Time

From flint arrowheads to fine woollens

by
Judi Thorpe
and
Mike Pinder

Published by Marsden History Group, www.marsdenhistory.co.uk

Design and layout, Keith Hemsley

Copyright 2014 - 2016 Marsden History Group

ISBN 978-0-9557175-4-3

All rights reserved. Apart from any fair dealing for research, private study or review no part of this publication many be reproduced, stored in a retrieval system or transmitted in any form or by any means without prior permission of the publishers who are the copyright holders.

Front cover illustration - Auction sale plan of Marsden Village centre c1870
West Yorkshire Archive
Back cover illustration - A boiler under construction at Taylors' Iron Foundry c1900
Marsden Photographic Archive

This book is dedicated to the memory of Leo Pennington who was an enthusiastic member of the Marsden History Group.

He was a true friend to each and every person he ever met and is sorely missed.

Acknowledgements

Many people helped us in the production of this book. We would like to thank them all for their encouragement and for sharing their knowledge and expertise. In particular we owe our gratitude to Colin Ellis for his help with the history and activities of the mills, to Alan Matthews for sharing with us his collection of local history material, the Saddleworth History Society for providing a scan of the 1854 Ordnance Survey map of the area and Nicholas Pollett who spent many hours editing it into useable form.

In researching the history of Marsden wherever possible we have used primary sources, many of which are held in the West Yorkshire Archives and the willing help given by the staff in both Huddersfield and Wakefield has been invaluable. In addition we are grateful to the Huddersfield and District Archaeological Society for their work in identifying the route of the Roman road within the area of the village and for allowing us to use images from their book on the subject. One of the authors, Granville Clay, has been a generous contact. The Huddersfield Canal Society has provided us with much research material and we thank them and, in particular, Bob Gough for his help with many enquiries and for allowing us access to the Geoff Brown Collection. Peter Fox of Saddleworth Museum, Tom Rayward at the Canal and River Trust and the staff and volunteers at the National Waterways Archive at Ellesmere Port who helped with sourcing maps.

Individuals such as Elizabeth Askham, Cynthia Phillips, Shirley Waterhouse, Amy Hansom, David Hall and Derek Pinder were helpful in responding to requests for information and for sharing their personal archives. Many of the old photographs throughout the book are drawn from the Marsden Photographic Archive and we would like to thank all those people who contributed to such a valuable historical resource. In particular we would like to thank the Colne Valley Museum for their permission to use two images from the Clifford Westerby Collection of Upper and Lower Bank Bottom Mills. The archive is still being added to and Roger Logue, Annie Dearman and Dave Smith have all provided modern photographs for the book. Thank you also to Alison Campbell for her donation of architectural drawings for shops properties on Carrs Road and Peel Street.

We would also like to thank the members of the Marsden History Group for their support and encouragement particularly Roger Logue, Wendy Jones and Hazel Seidel who also passed on important information that she came across during the course of her own research project. On a more practical level we are extremely grateful to the Cuckoo's Nest, our splendid local charity shop, for their financial help and to Steve Harrison for proof reading a draft of this book and for his helpful comments.

Foreword

Marsden has a rich heritage. It has been a Pennine crossroads since hunter gatherers of the Mesolithic Age 9000 years ago tramped across the moors. The Romans built a road through it, linking York to Chester, packhorse tracks traversed the hills into Lancashire, turnpike roads followed. Standedge got a canal as well as three railway tunnels.

Any 'journey through time' needs facts, figures and explanations and the authors present an assiduously researched history, along with maps, illustrations and emotive photographs. They also add fascinating sidenotes and reveal forgotten secrets that bring the past vividly to life.

Learn about the Standedge Admiral and how Blind Jack of Knaresborough, famous road builder of his day, built a turnpike across marsh ground by binding the foundations with layers of heather: people still use it, 140 years later.

Discover why the old burial ground in Towngate had to be raised in 1796 to accommodate 99 burials in one year and read how Dutch Harry became the last person to be sent to the stocks at the bottom of Towngate in 1820 for being drunk and disorderly. '*Harry was treated as a martyr and a hero and Marsden held high holiday, while Harry was liberally supplied with food and drink.*'

Marsden has always had strong characters and a strong identity because of its very location. This excellent and engrossing history explains why.

Denis Kilcommons

Contents

Introduction

The vibrant community of Marsden is important to the people who live in the village at the present time but many past generations of men, women and children have lived and worked here and have contributed to the growth, development and changes that have resulted in the village environment we see today.

The aim of this book is to trace Marsden's history, from the available evidence, and to identify how and why changes took place. We have concentrated on tracing the social and industrial history of three areas; the village centre, the New Mills site and the Wessenden/Carrs Road area. When combined, these three parts of the village illustrate the pattern of change that transformed Marsden from a remote rural settlement to an important industrial 'town' producing quality woollen cloth which was acknowledged worldwide.

The earliest evidence we have of people living in the area is from flint arrowheads and other tools found on the moors around Pule Hill, Warcock and March Hill, together with other evidence such as hearths and flint-working debris. These artefacts were left by people in Mesolithic times from about 7,000 BCE onwards. In addition, burial urns, two of which contained cremated human bones dating from the Bronze Age, were unearthed on Pule Hill. Many of these items can be seen at the Tolson Museum in Huddersfield.

Bronze Age urns in the Tolson Museum collection

We have little or no further evidence of human activity until the building of the Roman road in about 79 AD connecting Chester with York via forts at Castleshaw in Saddleworth and Slack at Outlane. This road passed through the centre of Marsden and it is very likely that such a well-made route remained in use long after the Roman Legions withdrew.

It seems that Marsden remained a wild, largely unpopulated, area for hundreds of years. The Norman knight, Ilbert de Lacy, was awarded the land by William I in around 1068 for his loyality in defeating King Harold and he used the 8,500 or so acres that comprised his Marsden estate as a hunting ground. We also know that the area was used for the free grazing of livestock because, in 1190, the monks of Fountains Abbey held a Grant of Pasture 'at Marchesdene' for forty cows and thirty oxen. Ilbert de Lacy established his baronial seat in Pontefract Castle. Throughout its 800 year duration Marsden Manor never had a resident Lord and, hence, never had a Manor House, despite the fact that the 1616 farmhouse, at Highgate, near to the bottom of Old Mount Road is commonly known by this name.

As time passed more families started to live on the land. These settled subsistence farmers were granted copyhold leases which were perpetual and could be gifted, sold and mortgaged.

However, any change in ownership of the lease could only be made by first surrendering the property to the lord who transferred it to the new owner on payment of a fine. There were two other charges levied by the lord, an entry fine payable by any new tenant upon 'admission' and a heriot on the death of a tenant, a heriot originally being the deceased's best beast but later commuted to a cash payment. Marsden is unusual in that, for much of its history, it was occupied almost entirely by copyhold tenants. The advantages of holding land in perpetuity are great in that continuity is guaranteed and thus, investment in improvements to property or land, stay 'in the family'.

The development of Marsden as a community of people living and working together was extremely slow. In 1424 there were a mere 17 tenants living with their families in primitive dwellings scattered over the area. This figure had risen to 30 by 1480 and to 80 by 1591. The Hearth Tax returns of 1666 showed there to be 82 houses present in the manor. In 1628 a survey of Marsden manor was commissioned by the City of London so as to ascertain its sale value. Peter Whitehead has transcribed this lengthy document into modern English giving a vivid description of the Marsden area at that time. The survey states that dwellings were scattered,

'...some high up the valley side, some close to the river, as shelter and the fertility of the ground did allow them. The hills above are vast, stony, Moorish and barren. The grounds about them are enclosed into small fields ... and these enclosures are made more fertile by applying burnt limestone which has to be brought from as far as Pontefract and Knottingly about 20 miles away and yet the ground is so cold and backward that only grass, oats and peas can be grown. These people have a hard life and yet many of them are very wealthy. They live as it were within themselves and constantly enclose and improve land out of the rude mountains above them.'

The surveyor was unable to establish what the farmers had paid per acre for the land they occupied because they said that they did not know how much it was and they never accounted any land by the acre. The conclusion was that 'These are more subtle people than ignorant and are very fearful of losing their customary rights'. It could be said that the characteristics displayed by Marsdeners in 1628 still hold true today. Self-sufficiency, hard work, suspicion of outside authority and loyalty to each other are qualities that still feature strongly in local people.

The land that eventually formed the manor of Marsden was originally part of other manors in the wider area. It was not for nearly 300 years after Ilbert de Lacy took possession in around 1068 that it became a manor in its own right. The manor was held at different times by individuals, the Crown and, for a short time, the City of London. The process of converting copyhold to freehold was completed in 1922 and the last of the manor land was disposed of in 1955 to the National Trust in lieu of death duties owed by Sir Joseph Edward Radcliffe. His son, Sir Everard Joseph Pickford Radcliffe, was the last lord of the manor.

It has already been noted that the early residents of Marsden lived in scattered farms. However the nucleus of a village centre was established by the building of a chapel in Towngate sometime during the mid 1400s. It could accommodate over 300 worshippers which would appear to reflect the number of people living in Marsden as a whole at that time. Its presence meant that villagers no longer had to walk to Almondbury or Huddersfield for their Sunday worship although Marsden Parish Church was not licensed to perform marriages until 1843.

Marsden was divided by the River Colne into the parishes of Almondbury, south of the River Colne and Huddersfield, lying to the north of the River Colne, until 1888 when it was united to form one parish.

Houses dating from the early 1700s line the road at the top of Binn
Judi Thorpe 2013

The population of the village slowly increased and there are records of houses dating from the pre-industrial period, some of which still exist. A good example would be the housing lining the top part of Binn Road on the eastern side of the Wessenden Valley above Butterley Reservoir.

The lives of the villagers of Marsden, before the mills became the principal means of livelihood, were centred around farming and home-based spinning and weaving of woollen cloth involving the whole family working together. Their cloth was taken to fulling mills to have the nap raised mechanically. The first one in Marsden was located at Hey Green and was built when a petition of 42 villagers, dated 1709, prompted Robert France of Holmfirth to build a mill after he was promised that they would patronise it.

For a brief period cotton yarn was also produced in the village. The manufacture of cotton yarn in Marsden was always factory-based. Many of the mill buildings in existence today occupy the sites of mills that were built as cotton mills towards the end of the 18th century. These include the mills discussed in Chapter 3 and others, such as Clough Lea Mill (1798), Crow Hill Mill (1795) and Lingardswood Bottom Mill (1797). The majority of these small cotton mills were converted to wool within ten years or so. This marked the beginning of the industrialisation of woollen textiles production. The process was aided by an improvement in the movement of people, goods and raw materials with the coming of the Turnpike roads and the canal.

The early small mills were either demolished and the site redeveloped with larger mills or augmented by additional buildings to house the increasing mechanisation of every process in the production of woollen cloth. The pattern of changes that occurred during this process is illustrated in Chapter 4, which describes the mills on the Wessenden Brook resulting in the huge Bank Bottom Mill still present on the site. This growth and the coming of the railway changed the once rural village into an industrial one. The population of the village grew rapidly to meet the labour demands of the textile mills, reaching a peak of 5962 recorded in the 1921 census.

Chapter 1 describes the access into and out of the village which both allowed development to take place and constitute responses to changing needs. Chapter 2 tells the story of the changes which occurred in the centre of the village, showing how Towngate gave way to Peel Street as the main shopping area. Unfortunately many of the pre-industrial properties in the Towngate area were demolished following slum clearance in the late 1930s.

Intensive house building by speculative builders, mill owners and even the Co-op struggled to keep pace with demand during the period of rapid expansion. The local authority then took over responsibilty for providing housing. The building of large housing estates started in the inter-war years with the Woods Estate followed by Dirker and Netherley. In recent years house building has largely been the province of private contractors.

Clough Lea is a good example of the changes that have taken place over a period of some 200 years. A small mill was erected there in 1798, initially for the production of cotton yarn. After conversion to woollen textiles, the mill was added to until the area was filled with industrial buildings. Clough Lea Mill lies at the western end of Clough Lea Road which has pre-industrial cottages along its path.

Clough Lea Mills prior to demolition
David Hall

Clough Lea Mills c1950
David Hall

With the demise of the woollen trade the mill buildings were demolished in 2000 and the site used for the private housing estate present today. The photograph below was taken from Manchester Road looking north west. The Clough Lea Mill chimney is still present above the terrace of houses known as Clough Hey on Manchester Road.

Clough Lea
Judi Thorpe 2013

Much of the built environment of the village that we see today refers back to earlier times. We hope this book will provide an explanation, albeit incomplete, of how and why, for instance, roads, bridges, mills and houses are where they are today and of the developments that have occurred to effect the change in the nature of Marsden from the wild, uninhabited place it was into the busy, attractive village it is today.

Chapter 1 - Crossing the Pennines

Marsden lies on one of the shortest east-west crossings in the South Pennines and, because of this, has seen a concentration of successive paths, tracks, roads and other modes of transport passing through the Parish, from Mesolithic times to the building of the railway in the 19th century. The existence of these routes had much to do with the origins and growth of the village.

People have been visiting the upper Colne Valley since Early Mesolithic times, over 9,000 years ago. The first to come were hunter-gatherers who left traces such as flint-knapping sites, arrowheads and hearths on the high moors. The people probably came from lower-lying areas to hunt during the warmer months. During the 7,000 years before the Romans arrived, footpaths must have become well established. Unfortunately, we can have no way of knowing which of our existing roads and paths have their origins so far back, but surely some do.

The Roman Road

The Roman road ran from Chester to York via forts at Castleshaw in Saddleworth and Slack at Outlane. Huddersfield and District Archaeological Society (HDAS) have carried out a long term study of the road and have found evidence for a large part of its route through the Marsden Parish. Coming from the west, the road entered the area from Standedge, over Thieves Clough and past Gilberts to Worlow, where there was a small fort or signal station. From here it ran along the east side of Pule Hill to a point south-west of High Gate, where it is lost due to quarrying activities. Thereafter, its course has not been discovered until it reaches Wood Nook, West Slaithwaite, but HDAS have proposed two possible routes, which are of necessity both generalised and speculative.

The proposed routes diverge at a point just north of High Gate. **Route 1** then drops down the steep hillside and follows the present footpath down the west side of the churchyard. However, it should be noted that this path was moved from its original position when the new Parish Church was built at the end of the 19th century. It originally lined up with the old humpbacked Mellor's Bridge. Route 1 then crosses the River Colne and continues up the hill, across Station Road and the railway and on via Ashton Binn to join route 2 just north of Sparth.

Route 2 drops down from High Gate to Throstle Nest, down Towngate and across the river to follow Warehouse Hill and Marsden Lane to Sparth. Both routes converge north-east of Sparth, between Marsden and Slaithwaite. HDAS are continuing with their work on the Roman road, and no doubt will fill in some of this gap in the route, but the subsequent heavy disturbance of the village centre by developments such as the canal, the railway and the expansion of industrial sites has made this task much more difficult.

Some practical comments can be made about the two routes in relation to the topography of the area; bearing in mind the fact that Roman road builders were practical and pragmatic. Both routes start with a steep descent from High Gate. Having crossed the River Colne, Route 1 takes a relatively gentle climb up to Ashton Binn, after which it is faced with a very steep drop down to the eastern ends of Green Hill and Park Gate Cloughs on its way to Wood Nook. It seems perverse to climb up so high on the side of the valley, only to drop down again. Route 2 has a much easier course, with no major obstacles. Its route, into what is now the village, is likely to remain a mystery, but it is not impossible that the ancient track which meanders down to Throstle Nest from High Gate is a relic of the Roman road.

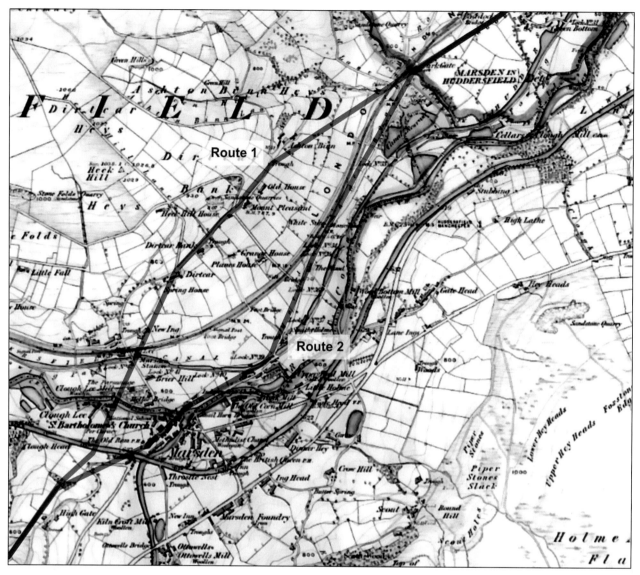

Alternative routes for the Roman road through Marsden, superimposed on the 6" 1854 O.S.map
Information from Huddersfield & District Archaeological Society

The route still has to cross the two streams from Green Hill and Park Gate Cloughs, but does so where they meet the flatter land of the valley bottom, where crossing would be much easier and no steep descents and ascents would be necessary. Although Route 2 runs at a much lower level than Route 1, it is still above the flood level of the Colne.

Exactly where the road crossed the River Colne and perhaps the Wessenden Brook is another mystery. Union Bridge and Snail Horn Bridge are known to have been the sites of fords or crossing places before the bridges were built, and the same may well be true of Towngate Bridge and Mellor's Bridge. Such crossing places would almost certainly have been in use long before the Roman road builders arrived and they would have appropriated those that served their needs.

It seems very unlikely that such a well-made road would be abandoned once the Roman armies ceased to use it after about AD140. It would have been of importance to the indigenous population and, as we shall see, there is some evidence for this.

Crossing the Pennines

Medieval roads

From early in the Middle Ages, Marsden was part of the Honour of Pontefract held by the de Lacy family. A developed village centre did not then exist. The district was de Lacy's hunting preserve and such tenants as resided within the area were required to escort their lord to and from his castle at Pontefract whenever he visited. The route they took is very likely to have been that taken by the present Meltham Road. This was probably also the route for the parishioners of Marsden-in-Almondbury to reach their parish church at Almondbury, on their way to major church events in their lives such as baptisms and marriages.

Warehouse Hill and Marsden Lane form part of the medieval road north east out of Marsden. This would probably have been the route taken by the parishioners of Marsden-in-Huddersfield to their parish church. It was also the principle route to Halifax and, although hard to read, it appears to be called Halifax Road in the Marsden-in-Huddersfield Township Map of 1801.

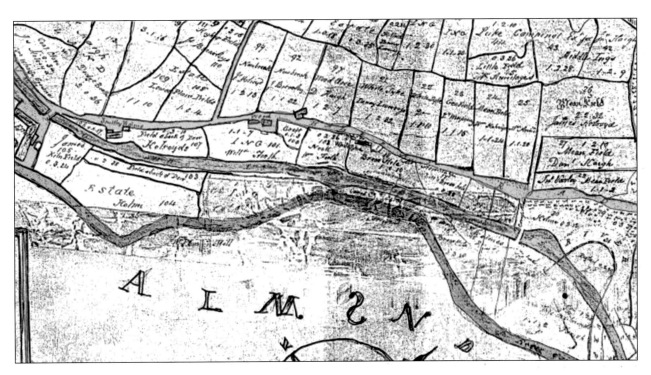

Detail from the Marsden-in-Huddersfield Township Map 1801 showing Halifax Road.
The bridge over the canal at Warehouse Hill is at far left.

If the Roman road did indeed follow the course of Marsden Lane, then it would be an obvious route for later people to use. Travelling eastwards from the village, Warehouse Hill and Marsden Lane nowadays seem to follow their original course to Sparth, with only a minor deviation at the top of Warehouse Hill caused by the building of the canal.

From Sparth, however, the road formerly veered northward and ran up the slope towards Slaithwaite Hall. When the railway was built in the late 1840s, it cut through the old road, and the railway builders provided an archway under the tracks to maintain access to the route, and to the farms higher up the slope.

Crossing the Pennines

Detail of Christopher Greenwood's Map of Yorkshire 1818 showing the old course of Marsden Lane from the village centre (bottom left) to Slaithwaite Hall (top right). The fact that the road is clearly shown suggests that it was considered to be an important route.

Marsden Lane nowadays continues as Park Gate Road, parallel to the railway, but this was not yet present when the 1854 O.S. map was surveyed. It was probably the coming of the railway which caused the building of Park Gate Road, extending Marsden Lane towards Slaithwaite. This route would have been much easier, and Slaithwaite Hall had by this time diminished in importance, so the old road fell into disuse.

It is now a footpath, but the first stretch from the railway arch is still a wide track and, where it crosses the stream issuing from Park Gate Clough, it does so on a wide and well-made stone bridge. This may or may not predate the railway, but in any case it is an indication of the former importance of the road.

The bridge over the stream at the bottom of Park Gate Clough.
Judi Thorpe 2013

The footpath up to Slaithwaite Hall, all that remains of the old Halifax Road at this point.
Judi Thorpe 2013

Crossing the Pennines

Overlooking the south-western side of the village from Pule Hill above Throstle Nest stands a farmhouse called High Gate, which carries a datestone from 1616.

The name simply means 'High Road', and the house was built next to what was then an important route to and from Marsden. From Towngate and Throstle Nest, the road climbed up the steep slope to where the property now stands; via the winding track already suggested as a course for the Roman road. This part still exists in the form of a rather overgrown public footpath.

High Gate from the south.
Marsden Photographic Archive

From High Gate southwards, the route must have been approximately parallel to Old Mount Road, but higher up the slope, The known course of the Roman road is close by, and a packhorse track certainly utilised at least part of this (see page 21). Other roads of medieval or earlier origin are probably still in use, but we have no evidence.

High Gate seen from the north-east. The old sunken roadway can be seen winding up
towards the house from bottom right. The modern access track is the pale one to the left.
Judi Thorpe 2013

Crossing the Pennines

The Packhorse ways

As the population of the Colne Valley increased along with the amount of trade, more efficient means of transport became necessary. Crump, in his book *Huddersfield Highways Down the Ages*, says that the packhorse roads developed in the 17th century, with the growth in the textile trade. Although this seems to have been when the practice of transporting goods using strings of packhorses or mules began to be commonplace, it is unlikely that these tracks were new creations; rather, it seems reasonable to assume a medieval or even earlier origin. They were, however, better maintained, and were often called 'causeys' reflecting the fact that they were paved with stone to give the animals a firm path on which to walk, regardless of the weather. The packhorses were taken in lines or 'gangs', the lead horse carrying one or more bells on its collar. Each animal had an arched saddle, sometimes padded, over which were slung a pair of containers - baskets, sacks or barrels. Some items of packhorse harness can be seen at the Folk Museum at Shibden Hall in Halifax.

Marsden seems to have been at the meeting point of several such routes. The Marsden to Rochdale packhorse road is the best known of those in the Parish, and still exists as a footpath, now forming part of the modern Station to Station Walk from Marsden to Diggle. Formerly known as Rapes Highway or Owd Rapes Gate, the name comes from the fact that it crosses part of Rapes Moor just beyond the Marsden boundary near the present A640 road to Rochdale. It is named Rapes Highway at this point on the 1854 O.S. map.

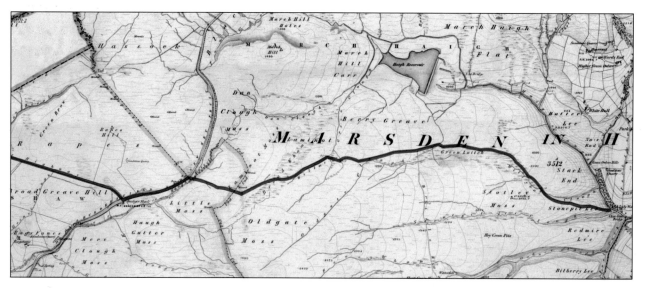

Detail of the 1854 O.S. map showing the route of the Packhorse Way from Eastergate Bridge to Rapes Moor. The route has been enhanced to make it more visible.

Traffic heading for Rochdale from the direction of Halifax or Huddersfield probably entered Marsden along Marsden Lane. From the point where the modern Union Bridge stands up to Hey Green, and perhaps as far as Eastergate, the track ran along the river bed itself. The weirs which obstruct the river bed were probably all constructed in the late 18th century.

Crossing the Pennines

It is not known when Eastergate Bridge and the streamside path running up to it from Hey Green were built. From Eastergate Bridge, the track climbed up over to Badger Slack, and from there it continued on over Rapes Moss towards Rochdale. The route is clearly marked as a track or footpath on the 1854 O.S. 6" map, and on later surveys, but does not appear on any of the earlier maps such as Jefferys', Greenwood's or Teesdale's.

The Packhorse Way served a variety of functions. Cloth, coal, seed, flour and other goods were transported in one or other direction, the traders aiming to have their animals fully laden in both directions.

An old view of Eastergate Bridge.
Marsden Photographic Archive

It was also used to gain access to the rush beds, and for carrying turf cuttings back from the peat beds as well as by sheep and cattle drovers taking livestock to markets in Lancashire. Most of this information comes from the evidence given by local witnesses at the Right of Way court case in Leeds in 1908. These witnesses were elderly residents of Marsden, whose memories stretched well back into the 19th century.

The witnesses in the Packhorse Road Trial in April 1908, photographed at Marsden Station.

Standing, left to right: James Schofield, Matthew Waterhouse, Robert Garside, Edwin Sykes, George Fielding, James Schofield, Joseph Kershaw, James Carter. Seated, left to right: John Whitehead, James Haigh, Sam Schofield, Benjamin Schofield, Samuel Shaw, William Bolton.
Marsden Photographic Archive

Crossing the Pennines

Another track, which is still in existence and is likely to have been used for packhorse traffic, runs down the valley from Wessenden Head into Marsden.

A modern footpath now follows a similar course to that shown on the 1854 O.S. map, with several deviations caused by the building of Wessenden Head, Wessenden, Blakeley and Butterley Reservoirs. It ran directly from Wessenden Head down to Binn Road and on via Fall Lane, Weirside and Argyle Street to Snail Horn Bridge at the bottom of Peel Street. There is little doubt that the route is ancient.

A postcard from about 1925 showing the footpath in the upper Wessenden Valley, probably at Great Hey. The track had been moved uphill at this point, following the enlargement of Wessenden Resevoir. Marsden Photographic Archive.

A further probable packhorse track runs from north of New Hey Road, past Cupwith Reservoir to Dirker Heys and then becomes Huck Hill Lane, before dropping down to Rough Lee. Also from the north, another track runs down from Buckstones House on New Hey road to Higher Green Owlers. This is shown as a track on the 1854 map and is still a public footpath. From here, it continues as a road downhill to Lower Green Owlers, then on to Hey Green to join the Rapes route. Meltham Road is another route very likely to have been used for packhorse traffic.

As a result of their Roman road investigations, HDAS have shown the existence of another packhorse way. Part of the Roman Road, running along the east side of Pule Hill was found to have been used and maintained as a packhorse track. This was presumably the high road or High Gate, and it seems more than likely that the Roman road was still being used as a trans-Pennine route over 1,000 years after the end of the Roman occupation.

The packhorse 'causey' laid over the Roman road on Pule Hill. Photo courtesy of Huddersfield & District Archaeological Society.

Crossing the Pennines

The Turnpike roads

The continuing increase in population and the growth in the textile trade through the 18th century, together with the increased use of wheeled traffic to transport goods, put the existing roads and tracks under increasing pressure. One solution to the problem was the building of the Huddersfield to Ashton canal, and the other was the making of the Turnpike Road.

A frustrating aspect of researching the evolution of the road system through Marsden is the lack of an accurate record, not only of the practicalities of their building but also the precise route taken at various times. We have to rely for most of our information on the evidence given by Crump in *Huddersfield Highways Down the Ages* and Whitehead in *Bygone Marsden*, much of which it is now impossible to verify. A lot may be inferred, however, from the study of the older maps, and of the topography itself. Following Crump, it has become the practice to refer to the First, Second and Third Turnpikes. This may not be helpful in understanding what was, in fact, the evolution of a single Turnpike from Wakefield to Austerlands over forty or fifty years, under the auspices of a single Turnpike Trust.

The Wakefield to Austerlands Turnpike Trust was responsible for the road and their rather grand name needs some explanation. In the 18th century it was customary for turnpike trustees to restrict their activities to their own counties. The equivalent trust on the Lancashire side of the border had already constructed a road from Manchester and Oldham in 1735, which terminated at Austerlands, on the then Yorkshire boundary south-west of Dobcross. It was therefore logical to make the new turnpike join up with this road. An Act of Parliament passed in 1758 enabled the Trustees to commence work on the new road. Turnpike roads were not constructed wholesale along new routes, but were mainly adaptations and improvements of existing roads. These might be widened or smoothed out and the road surface improved to make them better suited to the increased traffic. Only where there was no alternative was a new route pioneered.

Detail of Thomas Jefferys' map of Yorkshire 1777 showing the route through the village.

Crossing the Pennines

The route through Marsden

The new Turnpike entered Marsden from Crosland Moor via Holt Head along Meltham Road to Chain. From there the road sloped down to Gate Head before continuing into the village centre. The line taken from Chain to the village centre is not known for certain. Jefferys' map of 1771/2, although a little vague, shows the road very definitely passing though Gate Head, and following a line which approximates to Brougham Road and Market Place.

Kiln Lane was an ancient track which ran beside the river from below Gate Head into the village at the point where the bottom of Peel Street is now, but the Turnpike appears not to have followed it. The map only shows its eastern end branching off the Turnpike.

The road crossed the Wessenden Brook '*almost opposite the present church*' according to Crump. Jefferys' map gives no indication how this was done, either by a ford or a bridge, but the uninterrupted depiction of the road implies that there was a bridge rather than a ford. Once across the Wessenden Brook, the road turned left onto Towngate and then climbed up the very steep slope past Throstle Nest and along Old Mount Road, on the east side of Pule Hill to Mount Bar, where it now meets Mount Road. From here, the road ran past Gilberts and straight on to Thieves Bridge, following the course of the Roman road for most of the way.

Thieves Bridge is worthy of some comment. At a width of 12 feet (3.7m), it is narrower than the carriageway of the turnpike either side of it, which is about 30 feet (9.1m). Thus it may well predate the building of the turnpike, and Crump suggests a building date of about 1760, although Whitehead gives the same date for the completion of the whole Turnpike. The bridge may well be even older. From Thieves Bridge, the Turnpike deviated southwards over Standedge and down to Austerlands.

Thieves Bridge
Photo courtesy of Huddersfield & District Archaeological Society

Crossing the Pennines

What is now called Old Mount Road formed part of a completely new stretch of road from Throstle Nest to Standedge. John Metcalf, 'Blind Jack of Knaresborough', was contracted in the mid-1770s to construct the section from Blackmoorfoot to Standedge Foot, just over the watershed in Saddleworth, a distance of about nine miles (14.5km). This included the most challenging part of the route, taking a new road over the peat moorlands, which were referred to as 'marshes'. The worst section seems to have been that between Mount Bar, where Mount Road and Old Mount Road now meet, and Thieves Bridge. The Trustees wanted the new road dug out of the peat, down to bedrock, and built up from there. Metcalf had a better, cheaper method, but the Trustees insisted that he use their method. He only prevailed when he made a bold promise to remake the road in their way, at his own expense, if his method failed. He began with the half-mile section from Mount Bar to Gilberts.

Metcalf used about 60 men to level the ground, and then to lay bundles of heather in rows on the intended road, These were pressed well down, and then another layer laid on top, the bundles laid at right angles to the first layer. Metcalf's autobiography does not say how many layers were needed, but when he deemed the surface firm enough, stone and gravel were laid on top and the final road surface built up. Most of this section of his road is still in daily use, 140 years later.

This aerial view, probably taken in the 1960s, shows the section of road where Metcalf used his new method of road building.

Taken from above the junction of Mount Road and Old Mount Road, the turnpike runs diagonally from bottom right. Its line is interrupted by the third route (the A62) and by the disturbance around the Redbrook engine house used in constructing the canal tunnel, but it can be seen to continue on the moor beyond, on the same line as the tarmacked stretch.

Aerial view showing part of the First Turnpike route.
Geoff Brown Collection

Crossing the Pennines

From the beginning, the Trustees worked to improve their road in a piecemeal way. Meltham Road has at some time been rerouted slightly at the Marsden end; it is obvious from the alignment of the old houses at Badger Gate, Badger Hey and Chain that they were built alongside an earlier road.

Unfortunately, the date of these houses does not help us resolve the date of the re-routing. The current road was either built as part of the original Turnpike route, or was built later to improve upon the pre-existing one. The lettering style on the nearby mile stone (see page 28) does not help us either. It could be from any time around the late 18th or early 19th centuries. The two routes converge at Chain, as can be seen on the 1854 O.S. map.

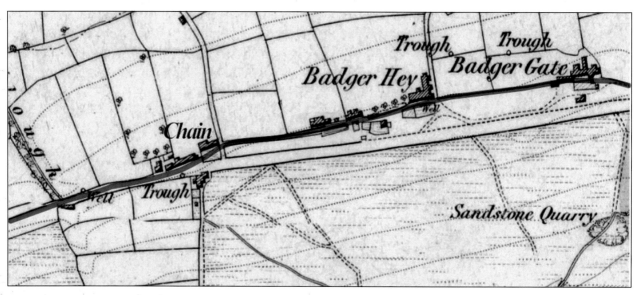

Detail from 1854 O.S. map showing the old line of Meltham Road from Chain eastwards. Some names have been edited out for the sake of clarity

Once the Turnpike was in use, it became clear that the steep climb, via Old Mount Road, up the side of Pule Hill from Towngate, especially the first section past Throstle Nest, posed a serious obstacle to wheeled traffic. The solution was a new stretch of road, forming Carrs Road and Mount Road, crossing over the Wessenden Brook via Ottiwells Bridge. Whitehead gives 1777 for completion of the bridge but, according to 'The Life of John Metcalf', he was contracted at some time between 1779 and 1781 to make this new section. He describes Ottiwells Bridge as 'twelve yards in the span and nine yards in breadth'. The bridge remains in use today, although it has recently been heavily reinforced.

The building of this section of the Turnpike must have had a drastic effect on Marsden, since it meant that traffic no longer needed to enter the village centre. The inns and other traders in Town Gate must have suffered loss of business, especially after new inns were built along Carrs and Mount Roads. Another major improvement was a new route from Mount Bar, across Warcock Hill and around the south side of Redbrook Reservoir to Standedge. This is not shown on a 1794 map of the proposed canal between Huddersfield and Ashton-under-Lyne, but is clearly in place on Christopher Greenwood's map of 1818.

Crossing the Pennines

Another problematic section was the route down into the village centre from Chain through Gatehead, which must have been both narrow and steep in places. Although most of the original route remains as lanes and tracks along this section, there is no obvious evidence on the ground to show what route the road took from Chain to Gatehead.

There is a road shown on Greenwood's map which branches off the Turnpike somewhere near Gatehead and runs down into the beginning of Kiln Lane. If the map is accurate, this road has disappeared. What is now the continuation of Meltham Road, which bypasses Gatehead, must have been built or enlarged to improve this stretch and lead straight into Brougham Road. It is of interest that the property called Steep Farm, with a date stone of 1773, is built directly adjacent to this newer route. Jefferys' map showing the original route through Gatehead was surveyed between 1767 and 1770, which suggests that this improvement may have happened very early.

The road marked in green running across from east to south west shows the new route along Carrs Road and Mount Road.

The earlier route along Brougham Road, Towngate and Old Mount Road is shown in pink.

Note - the road shown in red may have formed the earlier route into the village via Gatehead.

Detail of Christopher Greenwood's map 1818

The Trustees continued their improvements over the years, but an Act of Parliament of 1820 enabled them to reroute their road considerably, and the result could justifiably be thought of as a new Turnpike. They had already begun to build the present Manchester Road along the Colne valley by this date, and another major rerouting was to take the road around the north and west sides of Pule Hill, crossing Metcalf's road at Gilberts, and driving a cutting over the summit at Standedge which severed the second route.

Major civil engineering was necessary throughout the length of the new route from Longroyd Bridge to Standedge cutting. Within Marsden itself, the road had to be raised to allow it to be carried over Fall Lane and the Wessenden Brook on two new bridges. As a consequence, the southern end of Oliver Lane was blocked off to wheeled traffic by a retaining wall. A flight of stone steps were provided to give pedestrians access to the new road, and these remain in use today.

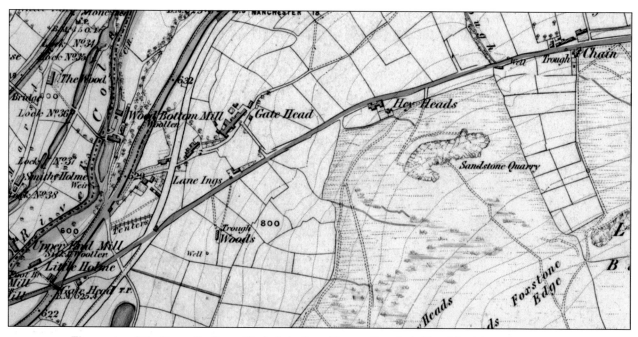

The route of the Turnpike from Chain into the village, after Gate Head had been bypassed.
There is no sign of the previous route from Chain to Gate Head.
Detail from the 1854 O.S. map.

By October 1838 the new road appears to have been satisfactorily completed as far as Cellars Cough. However, a group of angry travellers wrote to the Leeds Mercury that month to complain about the state of the section from there into the village. It is clear that their complaint related to Stubbin Road, from Cellars Clough to its junction with Meltham Road. The response of the Turnpike Trust was to ask for their patience, since all available resources were being ploughed into completing the new route, which would include a new section from Cellars Clough into Marsden.

What route was followed from Meltham Road onwards remains a mystery, but since the whole new Turnpike was opened only ten months later on 10th August 1839, a large part of the remaining work must have been done already. The fact that the new road severed the second route at Standedge cutting would have put that route out of commission some time before the new one was complete.

It seems likely that a temporary bridge was built to straddle the new cutting or, perhaps John Metcalf's original Standedge crossing was pressed into service for a few weeks.

A late 19th century view of Standedge cutting, looking towards Marsden from approximately the point where the Turnpike cut through the second route over Standedge.
Marsden Photographic Archive

Crossing the Pennines

The new route was well suited to fast, wheeled traffic such as the mail coaches and, with little alteration, it served as one of the major trunk routes over the Pennines, carrying large amounts of heavy commercial traffic until the opening of the M62 in 1971. After that, traffic through Marsden was drastically reduced.

The Turnpike Trusts were profit making enterprises, and their income was derived from the tolls they charged. These were carefully worked out to compensate for the likely wear and tear on the road surface caused by the different types of traffic. Small livestock like sheep were charged least; vehicles drawn by various animals were charged for each animal, as well as being charged according to the width of the 'fellies' or wheel rims. The wider the fellies, the lower the charge, presumably on the basis that narrow wheels were more likely to dig in and damage the road surface. Once they arrived on the scene, steam-powered vehicles were charged far more heavily than anything else. As a result of the Local Government Act of 1888, tolls were abolished and responsibility for maintaining main roads was given to county councils and county borough councils.

The tolls were collected at toll gates or bars, where road users paid for their journeys. These were normally accompanied by houses for the toll collectors and their families. A toll gate is shown on the Marsden-in-Almondbury Tithe map of 1848 spanning the crossroads at the junction of Manchester Road and Brougham Road/Meltham Road near Green Bower, where the 1841 census shows one John Kaye as toll collector. Another at the junction of Meltham Road and Stubbin Road is probably the Gate Head Bar referred to as the dwelling of Robert Barrett and James Carter, toll collectors, in the 1851 census. Lines extending across the road indicate the toll gates.

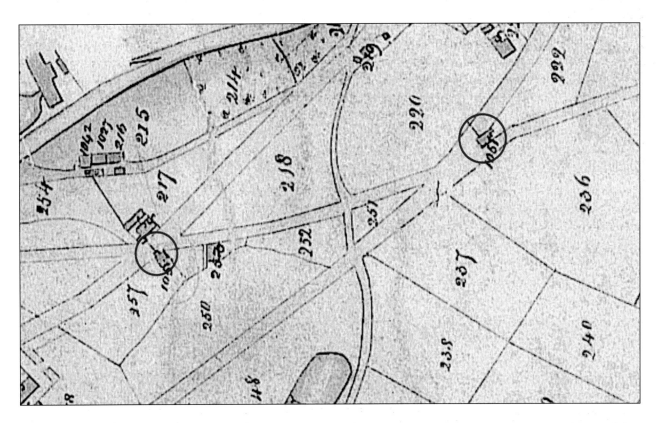

Detail from the Marsden-in-Almondbury Tithe map 1848, Manchester Road runs from top centre to bottom left, with Meltham Road and Brougham road running across the middle. The toll bar at the junction of Stubbin Road and Meltham Road is at the right, and another can be seen at the main crossroads with Manchester Road at left centre.

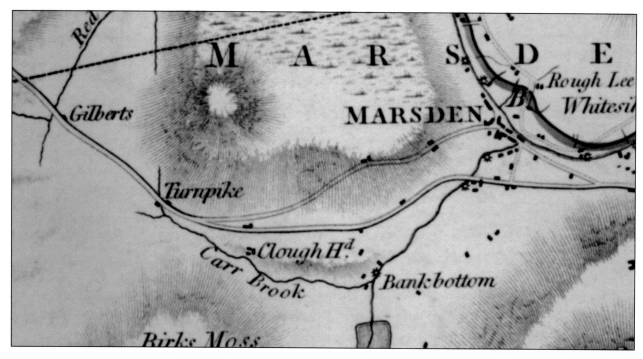

Detail from a map of the route of the canal between Huddersfield and Ashton-under-Lyne 1794

Gilberts is often referred to in the literature as the site of another toll bar, but the Tithe map does not show it. However, a map made to show the route of the proposed canal in 1795 has the word 'Turnpike' next to a building to the west of the junction of Old Mount Road and Mount Road, opposite to where Old Bridge House then stood. It is not clear whether the mapmakers were simply indicating that they were showing a turnpike road, or that this was the position of the Turnpike itself, i.e. the toll bar. No others are shown in Marsden.

Another feature of Turnpike Roads was the provision of mileposts or milestones along the route, with the mileages from each end of the Turnpike displayed on them.

The two sides of the of Turnpike milestone at Badger Gate, Meltham Road. The inscriptions have been chalked in to make them more visible (to Austerlands 9 miles and to Huddersfield 6 miles). Roger Logue 2012

Crossing the Pennines

Other Turnpikes

The Wakefield to Austerlands Turnpike had by far the biggest effect on the village, but two other turnpikes skirted the parish and opened up other routes for trade.

The Huddersfield to New Hey Turnpike Trust Act was passed in 1806, enabling the building of what is now the A640 road from Huddersfield via Outlane to Rochdale, or the Nont Sarah's road as it is known locally. This runs north of Slaithwaite Moor and Cupwith Hill to March Hill, where it passes Buckstones House as it swings around above March Haigh Reservoir.

Although there is no straightforward way for modern traffic to descend from the Turnpike towards Marsden, in the days when goods were carried by man and beast, there were several tracks down from the road, including the Rapes Highway and two other probable packhorse tracks (see page 20).

That at least one of these was in regular use is indicated by a milestone at the Lower Royal George Inn, Scammonden. It indicates Marsden, but unfortunately the mileage has now been weathered away or broken off.

**Mile stone near the Lower Royal George, Scammonden.
Annie Dearman 2011**

Isle of Skye Hotel, Meltham & Marsden Moors, 1,477 Ft. above Sea level.

The Isle of Skye Hotel, Wessenden Head.
Marsden Photographic Archive

The Greenfield to Shepley Lane End Turnpike Act was passed in 1823 or 1824. This Turnpike now forms the A635 Greenfield Road from Holmfirth, which runs just south of the Marsden parish boundary at Wessenden Head. It was met by the ancient track up the Wessenden Valley at about the site of the now demolished Isle of Skye Hotel, perhaps partly explaining the position of this very isolated hostelry.

Not only have the major transport routes brought business and social changes to the village, but Marsden's landscape has been much altered by their construction. To some extent, this began with the major works needed to build the third Turnpike route, with its cutting and embankments. The canal and especially the railway left even bigger marks on the scenery.

The most obvious of these are the four tunnels under Standedge, but the digging of these tunnels, and other works along the routes of the canal and railway caused other changes, including the various pieces of infrastructure they necessitated, as well as the placing of heaps of spoil at various sites, along with a number of quarries for the building stone that was required. The canal also caused the building of a number of reservoirs to supply it with water.

Crossing the Pennines

The Canal

On 17th May 1793, a meeting was held in Marsden in the house of Humphrey Dyson to discuss the idea of building a canal from Huddersfield to join the existing canal from Manchester to Ashton-under-Lyne. This set in train a process which led eventually to the building of the canal which is such a feature of Marsden today. The full story of the canal has been told in several publications, so the following is just a brief outline.

The route of the new canal was surveyed in 1794 and work began the following year. There were many problems during the building of the canal which extended the construction period until early 1811. Large-scale civil engineering was still a relatively new field and the boring of the Standedge tunnel was the major difficulty. There was a constant need to raise more finance, many of the locks had to be rebuilt because of poor workmanship and work on the tunnel itself eventually ground to a halt through poor management and lack of funds. The canal either side of the tunnel was completed, and trade began, with trans-Pennine cargoes having to be transferred to packhorses or wagons at Marsden for the journey over Standedge. Because it was now possible to transport bulk goods to and from the village, a warehouse became necessary, and this was built near Smithy Holme. The canal was built on the north side of the Colne, and the only access to it from the main part of the village was via a ford at the bottom of what is now Peel Street. Thus it was that Snail Horn Bridge was built in 1798/9, skewed towards the new warehouse.

Thomas Telford was hired in 1806 to make a survey of the existing works and to estimate the cost of completing them. Telford was already well known as a successful civil engineer working on canals and roads, and his very detailed report was presented to the shareholders the following year. He estimated that if his plan was adopted, the tunnel would be completed in December 1810, and on 10th December that year, the first boat passed through the whole length of Standedge Tunnel. To modern observers, the construction of the canal and especially the tunnel may seem to have taken an inordinately long time, but the ambition of the Canal Company was at the very limits of what was then possible.

Standedge Tunnel interior. This photograph shows the unlined and very uneven nature of most of the tunnel, which was excavated by the use of gunpowder blasting and manual labour.
Marsden Photographic Archive

The gradients either side of the tunnel are very steep for canal building, and the tunnel is still the longest, at the highest altitude and the deepest below ground of any on the entire British canal system.

Although originally planned to have a towpath running through the tunnel, this idea was abandoned some years after work started as a means of reducing costs, so boats had to be 'legged' through the tunnel. To do this, a plank was laid across the front of the boat on each end of which a man lay and walked his feet along the tunnel walls.

Crossing the Pennines

With a fully laden boat, this was hard physical work, not helped by the very uneven nature of the wall surface. The boat horses were detached at the tunnel mouth and led over the moors to the opposite end of the tunnel.

Thomas Bourne was appointed as the tunnel's first Traffic Regulator when the canal opened, at the age of only 12 years. His father John, a miner from Worcestershire, had worked on the tunnel construction before being appointed Tunnel Superintendent, and the family lived at 'Tunnel Mouth'. Thomas remained in his job for the next 37 years, earning the nickname 'The Standedge Admiral' in the process. Exactly what his job entailed is something of a mystery, but he had to cross over to the Diggle end four times a day, seven days a week. It seems likely that he took the boat horses to meet their boats at the other end of the tunnel, so he probably rode on one of them, but we have no proof of this. However he did it, he would encounter every kind of weather the Pennines could throw at him, and must have had a remarkable constitution. He also had to carry money, perhaps the fees collected from the boatmen for traversing the tunnel.

The evidence of the tunnel building is very obvious on the ground above its course, with spoil heaps by the ventilation shafts, and by the engine house at Redbrook. Other spoil from the tunnel was probably used along its route for building embankments. Reservoirs were needed to supply the canal with water, and those built within the Parish are at Black Moss, Swellands, Redbrook, March Haigh, Tunnel End and Sparth. Even with all these and other reservoirs, water supply was (and still is) a continuing problem because of the large number of locks with only short 'pounds' between many of them.

Water supply was also of vital importance to local manufacturers at a time when most mills were powered by water wheels, and the Canal Company was constantly having to reassure these people that their water supplies would not be threatened by the canal taking water for its own supply. Wessenden Reservoir was built in the 1790s by a group of local mill owners to ensure the water supply to the mills along the Wessenden Brook, but it is possible that its construction was a pre-emptive move, prompted by the proposal to build the canal.

Redbrook Engine House. This building was erected to house the engine which hoisted spoil up from the tunnel workings at the bottom of the shaft below. The picture was taken in 1959 from the top of the substantial spoil heap which was built up beside it, before conservation and safety work was carried out on the building. **Geoff Brown Collection**

Crossing the Pennines

The Navvies

In order to build a major undertaking such as the canal, a large number of labourers were required. From the building of the canal onwards, the presence of large numbers of such men was a regular feature of Marsden life until the completion of the third railway tunnel in 1894. They gained the name 'navvies' when they first appeared in the 18th century working on the canals or 'navigations'. While many local men would have gained useful income from this work, many more men would be needed. The tradition is that navvies were predominantly Irish, but we do not know whether Irish navvies worked in Marsden. We do know that Thomas Bourne's father came from Bewdley in Worcestershire to work on the canal tunnel, and we also know that a number of Welsh slate miners from Anglesey appear on the 1891 census living at Redbrook, among other sites on the moors, which coincides with work starting on the third railway tunnel.

Temporary accommodation would be set up for the navvies near the workings, and these could be quite substantial, given that the work could take years to complete. During the protracted digging of the canal tunnel, cottages were built close to the shafts at Redbrook and Flint Pits (on the west side of Pule Hill) as well as nine more at Gilberts, with vegetable plots for food. We have no images of this early accommodation, but we do have one of that which was built at Tunnel End for the men working on the third railway tunnel. The navvies left their mark in more ways than one; like Thomas Bourne's father, some settled in the area and raised families.

The wooden huts erected to accommodate some of the workers during the construction of the third railway tunnel. They were sited overlooking Tunnel End Reservoir at Ainsley.
Geoff Brown Collection

Crossing the Pennines

The canal was never a huge commercial success but was used for transporting bulky goods, especially along the Colne Valley. It continued in regular but declining use until the inter-war years. The last boat with a commercial cargo passed through the tunnel on November 6th 1921 at 6.30 pm, having taken four hours to make the passage. Traffic continued, but by the start of the Second World War, had dwindled to almost nothing and the tunnel was in a poor state. By this time, the canal was owned by the London Midland and Scottish Railway, and in 1944 they obtained an act of Parliament which enabled them to abandon the canal.

Eventually, all the locks were turned into cascades. Occasional trips through the tunnel were still made, the last of these being on April 1st 1967. A group of enthusiasts formed the Huddersfield Canal Society in the 1970s and set about clearing out the canal and restoring the locks to working order, with the ultimate ambition of reopening the canal along its entire length. Their dedication and persistence paid off in May 2001 when Standedge Tunnel, was reopened for traffic, with the official reopening of the canal the following September.

The reopening of Standedge tunnel by George Greener, Chairman of British Waterways, on 26th May 2001.
Alan Stopher

Crossing the Pennines

The Railway

From 1841, there was a trans-Pennine railway along the Calder Valley, but not only was this inconvenient for the people of Huddersfield, it was also a rather indirect and slow route for trade between Leeds and Manchester. This was a period of very rapid expansion in the railway system, and the Huddersfield & Manchester Railway & Canal Act was passed in April 1845, its title showing that from the railway's beginning, it was intended to take over the canal company. Although it might be supposed that the Company would discourage the use of the canal in favour of the railway, they did, in fact, maintain it for the next century, and trade along it continued.

The new company was authorised to begin building the line on 21st July the same year. Rapid progress was made, and the line through to Stalybridge opened on 1st August 1849. The new single-track railway tunnel took only three years to build which, by comparison with the time it took to build the canal tunnel, shows the rapid progress that had been made in civil engineering skills in the intervening years. A major advantage was the fact that the canal tunnel ran parallel to the new railway tunnel, and only a short distance below and to the west. This enabled adits to be cut between the tunnels so that spoil from the new workings could be loaded onto boats and taken away. These heavily laden boats would have to be legged out of the tunnel, a fact that reminds us of the strength and endurance of the men who worked on the railway tunnel.

Some timetables survive from the first year of operation on the new railway, which make interesting reading. One, published on 28th July 1849, shows that there were four trains a day from Huddersfield to Marsden and rather mysteriously, five in the other direction on weekdays, with three each way on Sundays. This had already increased to nine in each direction by November 1850. The trip took 21 - 25 minutes, stopping at Longwood, Golcar and Slaithwaite and single fares were 1s 2d (£0.06) first class, 10d (£0.04) second class and 7d (£0.03) third class.

DOWN TRAINS FROM LONDON, BIRMINGHAM, CHESTER, LIVERPOOL, MANCHESTER, &c.

Distnc. from Manch.	STATIONS.	WEEK DAYS.								SUNDAYS.			FARES from MANCHESTER.			
													Express 1st Class	First Class	Second Class	Third Class
—	LONDON .... Departure				6 15				6½ & 11 3 & 4½		10 0	7 0				
—	BIRMINGHAM ,,				7 38	9 45			5 30			3 0				
—	CHESTER ,,			7 0	8 52	11 0			5 45		12 35	6 15				
—	CREWE ,,			7 40												
—	MACCLESFIELD ,,			8 30	10 10	12 30	1 20	4 30	8 15	6 45	2 0	8 0				
—	STOCKPORT ,,			9 0		10 40			6 20			6 25	6 0	5 6	4 0	2 7½
—	LIVERPOOL ,,			7 0	9 0	10 40										
		1. 1,2,3 Class.	2. 1,2,3 Class.	3. 1,2 Class.	4. Express.	5. 1,2,3 Class.	6. 1,2 Class.	7. Express.	8. 1,2,3 Class.	1. 1,2,3 Class.	2. 1,2,3 Class.	3. 1,2,3 Class.	s. d.	s. d.	s. d.	s. d.
—	MANCHESTER, Victoria Station .... Departure	a.m.	a.m. 7 0	a.m. 8 40	a.m. 10 5	p.m. 12 35	p.m. 3 0	p.m. 5 40	p.m. 8 20	a.m. 8 5	p.m. 2 0	p.m. 8 15				
1½	Miles Platting		7 5			12 40			8 25	8 10	2 5	8 20		0 4	0 3	0 1½
2½	Park		7 8			12 43			8 28	8 13	2 8	8 23		0 4	0 3	0 2
3½	Clayton Bridge		7 11			12 46			8 31	8 16	2 11	8 26		0 6	0 4	0 3
5	Droylsden		7 15			12 50			8 35	8 20	2 15	8 30		0 9	0 6	0 6
6½	Ashton		7 20	9 5		12 55			8 40	8 25	2 20	8 35		1 0	0 9	0 6
8	STALEY BRIDGE		7 25		10 30	1 0	3 25	6 5	8 45	8 30	2 25	8 40		1 3	1 0	0 7½
10½	Mossley		7 33			1 8			8 53	8 38	2 33	8 48		2 9	2 1	1 4½
13	Greenfield		7 41			1 16			9 1	8 46	2 41	8 56		3 2	2 5	1 7
14½	SADDLEWORTH		7 47	9 22	10 42	1 22	3 42	6 17	9 7	8 52	2 47	9 2	4 3	3 5	2 7	1 8½
19½	MARSDEN		8 3	9 34		1 38	3 54		9 23	9 8	3 3	9 18		4 3	3 3	2 1½
21½	SLAITHWAITE		8 9	9 39		1 44	3 59		9 29	9 14	3 9	9 24		4 6	3 5	2 3½
23½	Golcar		8 17	9 45		1 52	4 5		9 37	9 22	3 17	9 32		4 11	3 9	2 5½
24½	Longwood		8 24			1 59			9 44	9 29	3 24	9 39		5 2	3 10	2 6½
26½	HUDDERSFIELD	7 15	8 30	9 55	11 5	2 5	4 15	6 40	9 50	9 33	3 28	9 45	6 6	5 3	4 0	2 8½
29	Bradley	7 21	8 36			2 11			9 56	9 41	3 36	9 51		5 6	4 5	2 11
30½	Heaton Lodge	7 27	8 42	10 5		2 17	4 25		10 0	9 47	3 42	9 57		6 0	4 6	3 0½
31½	MIRFIELD	7 32	8 47	10 10	11 15	2 22	4 29	6 50	10 7	9 52	3 47	10 2		6 0	4 9	3 1½
34½	DEWSBURY	7 42	8 57	10 18	11 25	2 32	4 38	6 57	10 17	10 2	3 57	10 12	8 0	6 6	5 0	3 4½
35½	Batley	7 46	9 1	10 21		2 36			10 26	10 11	4 6	10 21		6 6	5 3	3 5½
38½	Morley	7 55	9 10	10 21		2 45	4 50		10 30	10 15	4 10	10 25		7 3	5 6	3 8½
40½	Churwell	8 1	9 16	10 36		2 50			10 36	10 21	4 16	10 31		7 6	5 10	3 10½
42	Wortley	8 7	9 22			2 51			10 42	10 27	4 22	10 37		8 0	6 6	4 0
43½	LEEDS .... Arrival	8 15	9 30	10 45	11 45	3 5	5 5	7 15	10 50	10 35	4 30	10 45	10 0	8 0	6 0	4 0
	POOL (for Otley and Ilkley) .... Arrival	8 43		11 23		4 43			9 55							
	KNARESBRO'	9 6		11 43		5 6			9 55							
	HARROGATE	9 6		11 43		5 6			8 15							
	RIPON	9 53		12 10		5 33			8 15							
	THIRSK	10 0		12 30		6 5			8 35							

LUGGAGE.
For better Security, Passengers are requested to take Carpet Bags and small Packages inside the Carriage; and every Description of Luggage must be plainly and fully directed. The Weight allowed for First and Second Class is 100 lbs. each Passenger, and for Third Class 56 lbs. Nos. 3, 4, 5, 6, 7, and 8 Trains run in conjunction with Trains from Liverpool, &c.

Part of the timetable published in the Leeds Mercury on 28th July 1849

Crossing the Pennines

Express services were first class only, although a third class carriage was provided for servants travelling with their masters. In those days, third class carriages were open to the elements. The timetable showed connections to London from Leeds via Huddersfield, a journey which would take between 8 and 10 hours. The single fare from Leeds to London was 21s (£1.05) first class and 10s (£0.50) third class.

The station entrance and booking hall on the bridge spanning the canal and railway, probably taken in the 1920s.
Marsden Photographic Archive

The line was built above the village on the north side of the valley, and the station was constructed at the point where it crossed Pinfold Lane, later called Station Road. This crossed the line by means of a level crossing at the eastern end of the station. At a later stage, perhaps when the second tunnel was built, the road was diverted west at the Railway Inn and then on a bridge over the canal and the railway tracks to Reddisher Road. The station entrance and booking hall were built on this bridge, and the station became a major piece of infrastructure, with four platforms, canopies and waiting rooms. All of this was demolished in the late 1960s. The goods yard included a goods shed which is now the National Trust office, and coal chutes where what must have been huge amounts of coal were unloaded ready to be distributed to the mills and houses.

Remains of the coal chutes, taken in the 1980s .
Geoff Brown Collection

Adjacent to the goods yard was The Railway Iron Works which, in 1887, was occupied by Mellor Russell & Co. engineers, millwrights and ironfounders. There was also a trans-shipment warehouse which was built directly over the canal next to the station. This stood between the two bridges which still cross the canal by platform three. An earlier version of this building is marked on the 1854 O.S. map, built over a short branch of the canal in roughly the same position. We do not know when it was moved to its later position, but it was certainly before 1895.

Crossing the Pennines

Although the railway line up the Colne valley was double track, the fact that the first tunnel was only single track caused many problems. Effective signalling had yet to be developed and so a pilot engine was used to accompany each train, the idea being that this one locomotive embodied the right of way to trains in alternate directions. There were many accidents which were often reported in the Leeds Mercury in gory detail. Together with the rapid increase in traffic, these must have motivated the railway company to build the second tunnel.

The new tunnel was bored to the east of the first and once again the canal was used to remove the spoil from the workings. Work began in 1868 and the tunnel opened on 12th February 1871. The new tunnel enabled much more traffic to traverse the route in safety.

The second half of the 19th century saw a massive growth in manufacturing in Britain, a large part of which took place in the north of England. This growth included expansion of the textile trade in Marsden, as well as the Taylor brothers' foundry.

The railway was the most efficient means of bulk transport and the Marsden manufacturers used it extensively to bring in raw materials and such things as coal for the mill engines and iron ore for the foundry. The railway could also be used to ship manufactured goods out of the village and this probably enabled the foundry to produce bulkier and heavier items than was previously practicable.

Freight traffic continued to increase, as did the number of passenger trains, and heavy freight trains labouring up the steep inclines of the Colne valley caused delays to fast passenger trains between Leeds and Manchester. Thus it became necessary to double the width of the line to four tracks, and a new double-track tunnel was necessary. This massive piece of civil engineering began in 1890 and was completed in 1894.

This final double-width tunnel was built with its eastern portal between those of the canal tunnel and the first railway tunnel. The line of the new tunnel, however curved across to the west side of the canal tunnel before straightening out. The canal tunnel therefore had to be reinforced for some distance from its entrance in order to take the weight of the trains. Yet again, the canal came into heavy use for removing the spoil.

The three tunnels were in continuous use from 1894 until the late 1960s when the whole route was reduced to two tracks. This meant that the two single-track tunnels were closed and the later double-track tunnel now takes all the traffic.

A goods train entering Marsden station from Huddersfield in 1965.
Note the flower bed on the end of the central platforms.
Geoff Brown Collection

Crossing the Pennines

Participants in the Silver Trowel dinner held at The Great Western Inn at Standedge on the occasion of the opening of the third railway tunnel. The men appear to be managers, foremen and the like. The identity of the gentleman holding the trowel is unfortunately not known. Geoff Brown Collection

One of the consequences of digging four tunnels, each of which is over three miles long, was the production of a vast amount of waste material. As a consequence, spoil heaps have become a major landscape feature in Marsden and its surroundings. Fortunately, these have become covered in vegetation and most are no longer especially noticeable. As has been said, the spoil from the canal tunnel is most obvious outside the village at Redbrook and by the ventilation shafts.

The site of the new houses at High Lea and the rather pleasant wooded area which stretches between there and Tunnel End is largely composed of spoil. There is no sign of it or the railway on the Marsden-in-Almondbury Tithe Map issued in 1848, which must have been surveyed in 1846/7. The Marsden-in-Huddersfield Tithe Map, which appeared in 1850, does, however, show both the railway and the River Colne canalised into a straight course to provide a site for the dumping of spoil from the new railway tunnel.

From this, we can assume that it is made of spoil from the first railway tunnel. In order to accommodate the spoil heap, the Colne was canalised into a straight course alongside it. The top of this spoil heap later became used for railway sidings, but the only sign of that now is a buffer-stop at the eastern end, in the form of a large box made of wooden railway sleepers filled with earth.

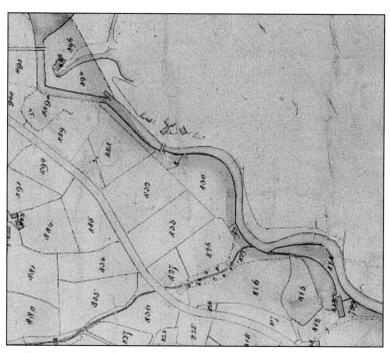

The area around the present Clough Lee spoil heap, as shown on the Marsden-in-Almondbury Tithe map of 1848 after the canal was built but before the railway. The River Colne is shown still following its ancient course.

Crossing the Pennines

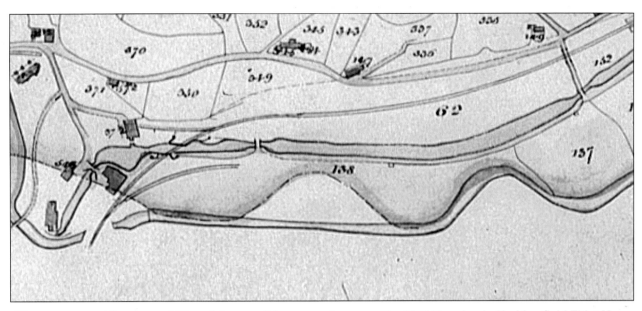

The area around the present Clough Lee spoil heap, as shown on the 1850 Marsden-in-Huddersfield Tithe Map.
The River Colne has now been partially canalised, but its old course
remains as the boundary between the two parishes.

Another spoil heap is at Warehouse Hill, between the canal and the railway. This was probably spoil from the third railway tunnel, since the 1895 O.S. map, surveyed in 1890, still shows field boundaries in this area which were obliterated by the spoil.

The ventilation shafts, which are a prominent feature of the moors above the tunnels, are usually accompanied by some sort of spoil, the most obvious from the village being those which can be seen on the skyline above Intake Head, near the memorial cross dedicated to the soldiers who served in World War II with the Duke of Wellington's West Riding regiment.

Because Marsden is situated in a fairly narrow valley, the village has been subjected to some major landscape changes. The fact that these all took place in the 18th and 19th centuries has allowed most of them to become covered in vegetation, or even built on, and so be absorbed into the landscape, to the extent that they can now be appreciated as enrichments of the scene and reminders of the ambition and enterprise of local people.

The remains of the old railway buffer stop above Clough
Lee mill pond.
Judi Thorpe 2013

Development of the Village Centre

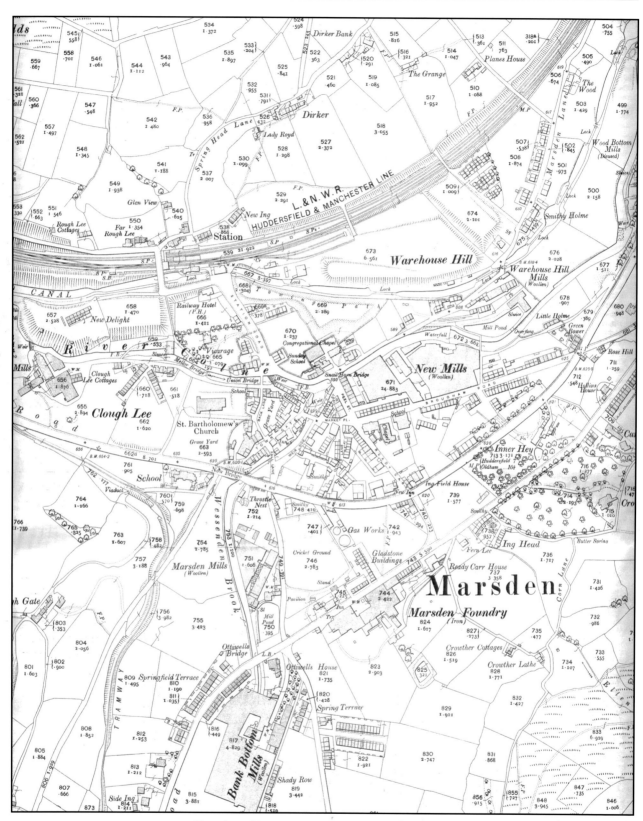

Marsden village centre, 25" to 1 mile O.S. 1904

Chapter 2 - Development of the Village Centre

St. Bartholomew's Church

Despite the fact that other buildings were known to be present at the time, Warburton's map of 1720 gives us no information about Marsden other than to show that there was a chapel present. This chapel-of-ease was built in the mid 1400s. It was built south of the River Colne and, thus, was in the parish of Almondbury. The building was of very basic construction with two doors which were, according to E. Irene Pearson in her history of the church in Marsden, "*so low that people entering the chapel had to stoop*" and "*when inside they could touch the roof*". It had accommodation for 311 worshippers. The position of the chapel within the township of Marsden established the nucleus of what, originally, was to become the centre of the village.

It is not known how or why this particular site was chosen for the church but it seems to indicate that it lay near to a trackway, which was in common use. By the mid 1750s the church building had become so dilapidated that it was decided to build a new church on the same site. It was completed in 1761 and was described as having three galleries and square pews. The floor was of bare earth so that people could have the privilege of being buried within its walls on payment of a fee.

In time this church building was felt to be unsatisfactory in many ways; the box pews made it almost impossible to kneel in prayer and there were complaints that the large number of bodies buried under the floor was insanitary.

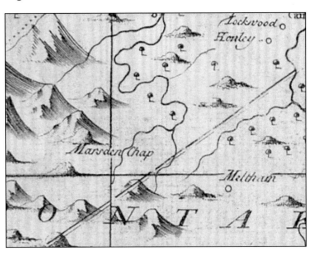

Extract of Warburton's 1720 map showing "Marsden Chap" near to the confluence of the River Colne and the Wessenden Brook.

Interior of the 1761 church showing the box pews, organ and stone columns supporting the upper galleries. Marsden Photographic Archive.

Development of the Village Centre

Although another site for a new church had already been acquired in 1852 it was not until 1865 that a building committee was formed to gather subscriptions and donations for a new church to be built.

The foundations for the new church on the opposite side of Church Lane were laid in 1866 but, due to a dispute with the building contractors, work was suspended and the old church continued to be used for worship for a further 30 years.

Photograph of Marsden's second church .
Marsden Photographic Archive

The old church became obsolete when services were transferred to the partly constructed new church. Tenders were invited to purchase the building material, '*in and about Marsden Old Church including taking down and clearing away*'. Francis Goodall's offer of £60 was accepted in February 1896 and soon after the building was demolished leaving only its footprint in Towngate.

The present parish church was built in stages re-starting in 1894 following extensive money-raising efforts. It was not completed until the tower, added in 1910, and the Baptistry, added in 1911, had been built. St. Bartholomew's Church is widely and affectionately known as the Cathedral of the Colne Valley.

The new St. Bartholomew's Church c1895 before the bell tower had been built.
Marsden Photographic Archive

Development of the Village Centre

The man in this photograph is standing inside the site of the old church which was surrounded on three sides by a burial ground. Planks is in the background. Marsden Photographic Archive

The village burial ground bordered the old church. There is a village story that Marsden was struck by a 'Black Death plague' in 1798. However, parish church burial records do not verify this. There was a peak of 99 recorded burials in 1796 but sadly the cause of death of these people is not given. The Huddersfield Examiner of August, 1863, reported '*It was in consequence of the extraordinary number of interments resulting from this visitation that the old graveyard became so overcrowded that it had to be raised artificially two or three feet above its original level; and the soil for this purpose was brought from the present footpath leading to Clough Lee which Daniel Haigh was then making by the river side and which path is known as 'The Weirside'. This elevation was the cause of the graveyard being considerably above the level of the pavement before the chapel door.*'

It is possible that the water available to householders was polluted, which could have caused outbreaks of typhoid fever. As late as 1863 the drainage in Towngate was discussed at a council meeting of the Marsden-in-Almondbury Board.

It was recorded that,
'*No action was taken. It involves the thorough drainage of the Towngate instead of the present system of open noxious sewerage and which will have to be grappled with if the world holds together.*'

Overcrowding in the graveyard became more and more of a problem. A new burial ground was created to surround the site proposed for the new church in 1852.

The site of the old graveyard showing Enoch Taylor's family tomb and the outline of the old church.
Judi Thorpe 2013

Development of the Village Centre

The old burial ground in Towngate was finally closed in 1897 although only free space in existing tombs had been used for many years. The old graveyard was deconsecrated and the site developed as a public recreational space in the 1970s. During the landscaping of the site the historical significance of Enoch Taylor, Marsden's famous iron-founder, was recognised. His tomb was preserved and moved to its present position near to the site of the old church. Wessen Court, sheltered housing built by the local authority, is at the far end of the old graveyard

Early Growth

The Hearth Tax returns of 1666 list all the dwellings in Marsden. At that time there were only 82 houses in the whole of the township and most people would have been living in houses scattered over the hillsides with enough land to grow their own food and, perhaps, keep livestock. A hearth was defined as a place on which you could boil a pot. There are two properties in Towngate still in existence today, which were present before Warburton's map was published. The White Hart Inn is traditionally believed to be the oldest public house in the village. The March 1911 edition of the Parish Magazine stated that the White Hart had a stone '*bearing the date 1590, which is now built into the wall, face inwards*'. This suggests that alterations to the inside of the building had interrupted an original entrance or that the stone had been reused from an earlier building. The inn was delicensed in 1910 and became a builder's store before being converted into a private dwelling in the 1970s. The property, adjacent to the White Hart, now No. 15 Towngate, is opposite the site of the old church.

Towngate on Fair Day c1880 showing the White Hart.
Marsden Photographic Archive

Development of the Village Centre

The second property in existence before Warburton's map was produced is No. 23 Towngate. At the rear of the house is a datestone carved with IH 1679 IH over a blocked-up doorway at first floor level. The ground floor opens onto the backyard and was originally used as stabling or a barn.

A close-up view of the date stone IH1679 IH
Judi Thorpe 2013

The rear of 23 Towngate with a carved date stone over the first floor entrance.
Judi Thorpe 2013

Thomas Jefferys surveyed the next map that we have with greater rigour between 1767-1770. It appears that his record of some buildings is symbolic rather than exact.

Jefferys appears not to show a building on the site of The Old Ram Inn at the top of Towngate, although it is believed to have been established around 1725. The inn stood on a path which linked Marsden with Saddleworth and beyond and was later developed as the first turnpike route. It was an extensive property and, when advertised for auction in the Leeds Mercury, dated 26th October, 1839, was described as

> **'All that old-established and well-accustomed INN or PUBLIC HOUSE, known by the Name of the Ram Inn, with the Brewhouse, Barn, Stables, Cowhouse, and other Outbuildings and Conveniences, with spacious Yards, well supplied with a never failing Spring of soft Water.'**

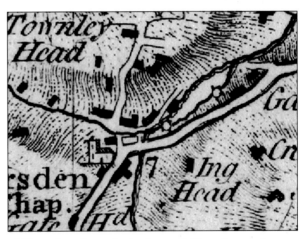

Although not precisely drawn Jeffreys' map shows the early development of the village centre in the 1760s

Development of the Village Centre

The Old Ram was situated on the route of the first Turnpike connecting Huddersfield with Manchester which ran up Towngate, the early hub of the village.

Marsden Photographic Archive

The Inn was also said to be '*contiguous to and near adjoining the new Diversion of the Wakefield and Austerlands Turnpike Road leading from Marsden to Delph*' (now the A62).

Coaches carrying goods, passengers and mail would halt at the Old Ram when travelling between Huddersfield and Manchester. The ascent up Old Mount Road was so precipitous that passengers would be invited to walk part of the way so as to relieve the horses. The property was demolished in 1926 along with the adjacent properties to make way for Towngate and Church Lane to be widened and for the churchyard to be extended.

The lower property, on the corner of Church Lane and Towngate, was a substantial house which was called The Chapel House and, later, The Hall. It is thought to have been built around 1756 and was the home of the Haigh family who imported poorhouse children to work in their mills. John Wesley is said to have once stayed the night at The Chapel House after having preached in Marsden.

The Chapel House, also known as The Hall is on the right-hand side of the photograph.
Marsden Photographic Archive

Development of the Village Centre

Behind The Chapel House was a yard, Chapel House Fold, containing several houses which were also demolished in 1926. One of these houses bore the date-stone 1683 RH.

Jefferys' map indicates that development had taken place in the centre of the village, principally in the Towngate area. There are a number of buildings indicated as being present in Towngate.

All the properties in Chapel House Fold were demolished soon after this photograph was taken. Marsden Photographic Archive

A large block of properties is shown on the opposite side of the road from the chapel which would have included the White Hart. The house immediately above the White Hart, now numbered 17 Towngate, has a date-stone SH 1738 HH inside the property over what was the original entrance. The property was extended at a later stage to form two cottages but which have now been joined to form one house. There is a replica date-stone displayed on the front of the building.

This date-stone is now over the old doorway inside No. 17 Towngate. Judi Thorpe 2012

A replica datestone has been incorporated into the front of the property. Judi Thorpe 2013

Following the 1930 Housing Act, which promoted the demolition of substandard housing, the council produced a Marsden Improvement Plan which led to the loss of many old houses in the centre of the village. Fortunately the datestones of the properties were recorded and show that, in addition to those mentioned above which are still present, there were several other houses in lower Towngate prior to 1771 namely, JK 1751 MK, BK 1752 MK and 1756 LF.

Development of the Village Centre

An alehouse called, intriguingly, The Two Dutchmen, stood at the bottom of Towngate facing across the bridge onto Market Place. Tradition has it that the building was originally built as a private house by two immigrants from Holland. They are remembered in the inn's name.

The Two Dutchmen closed in 1968 and was demolished soon afterwards. There is a datestone taken from the inn which shows two tulips and W 1762 B.

The property changed from being a private house to become an alehouse called The Two Dutchmen.
Marsden Photographic Archive

This stone has been placed on the grass near to the site of the old church and was salvaged by the people who developed the site as a recreational area.

'Dutch Harry', so called because he was the husband of the landlady of The Two Dutchman Inn, was the last person to be held in the stocks. The Huddersfield Examiner of 7th October, 1899, carried a nostalgia piece about the incident. On the evening of 11th November, 1820, Harry Broadbent had spent an evening celebrating the birth of his son by '*washing its head*' when he and his companions heard the foundry and factory bells clanging. They were being rung to celebrate Queen Caroline's success in preventing her '*worthless husband, George the Fourth*' from divorcing her. '*Harry determined to share in the rejoicings*' and having gained access to the church he '*seized the dangling rope*' and rang the bell for a full five minutes.

He was taken to court and found guilty of being drunk and disorderly. He refused to pay the fine and was punished by being ordered to spend six hours in the stocks.
'*Harry was treated as a martyr and a hero, and Marsden held high holiday, while Harry was liberally supplied with food and drink. When the term of his incarceration had expired Harry was carried in a chair on the shoulders of his friends in triumph.*' It is unlikely that others who were put in the stocks received such treatment from fellow villagers.

The stocks, shown in their original site at the corner of Church Lane and Towngate, were last used as a punishment in 1820.
Marsden Photographic Archive

Development of the Village Centre

The rear of cottages on Clough Lea taken from the Parochial Church Hall car park. Judi Thorpe 2013

Although not shown on the early maps of Marsden, it is apparent that Back Lane, later renamed Church Lane, was in use from an early date as a pathway around the old church building leading to the River Colne where, according to Whitehead, the river could be crossed by stepping-stones.

Clough Lea runs alongside the river past Mellor's Bridge and onwards up to a site which was first developed in 1798 when the original Clough Lea Mill was built.

There are several terraces of old cottages alongside the road which date from the late 1700s. One of the cottages bears a datestone JP 1782 SP. Clough Lea is also spelt Clough Lee, both are accepted as correct, although older Marsden residents use the more colloquial name of Clowley.

The Green lies on the opposite bank of the River Colne from Clough Lea. The row of cottages still present on the site is shown on Jefferys' map. One of them carries a modern plaque with the date 1763, which we believe to be correct.

Clough Lea datestone.
Judi Thorpe 2013

Prior to the building of the Congregationalist Chapel at Buckley Hill worship was conducted in one of these cottages.
Judi Thorpe 2012

Modern datestone 1763.
Judi Thorpe 2013

Development of the Village Centre

Middle Mill lay upstream of Mellor's Bridge.
Marsden Photographic Archive

To the west of the row of cottages stood Middle Mill which was built as a water-powered cotton mill in 1841 on the site of an earlier mill. The mill was demolished in 1996 and the site developed for housing.

Pinfold Lane, now called Station Road, is also clearly shown on Jefferys' map. The original line of the lane ran in front of the row of old cottages and a relic of this old lane is still evident. The modern Station Road was created slightly to the east of the old lane to better serve the traffic to and from the railway station which opened in 1849. This road originally continued straight up the hillside via a level crossing. In the late 19th century a bridge was built over the railway lines and the road was diverted to follow its present-day course. Part of the high curved wall which formed the pinfold is still present in the garden of one of the cottages visible from the bottom of Station Road. Stray animals were rounded up by the Pinder and held in the Pinfold until they were released to their owners on payment of a fine.

The original pathway which ran up the hill is still present in front of these cottages at the foot of Station Road.
Judi Thorpe 2012

The Pinfold was a large circular compound surrounded by a high wall. Part of this wall now forms the boundary to a garden.
Judi Thorpe 2012

Development of the Village Centre

Pinfold Lane is named on later maps as continuing down in front of the properties where the Swan Public House now stands. Despite its more modern frontage the Swan, when seen from its backyard, is an old building and may be one of the buildings that Jefferys shows on this site.

A footbridge crosses the River Colne near to the Swan Public House and originally led to the area of housing called Planks. An old photograph of Planks shows a house with a datestone 1744 EB MB. It has been partly chiselled away however and appears to have been recycled from another building although it is probable that the original property was built nearby.

An old date-stone built into a house in Planks.
Marsden Photographic Archive

Planks was two streets of old houses built sometime in the mid 1700s. Whitehead, writing in 1942, described Planks as being composed of '*two narrow streets with a picturesque turn at the west end and a quaint archway over a foot passage at the other*'.

Whitehead went on to say that Planks was '*built for its whole length over a conduit with its twin sister, The Street or Golden Alley, running parallel*'. The conduit is the goit which served to supply the reservoir on the New Mill site.

Planks was demolished during the late 1930s as part of the slum clearance programme. The site remained a waste area until the mid 1960s when the council built Wessen Court, a sheltered housing complex, on virtually the same footprint as the older properties.

A footbridge linking Station Road with Planks, now the site of Wessen Court,
may have existed for at least 250 years.
Marsden Photographic Archive

Development of the Village Centre

There were several established pathways which converged on the centre of the village before the building of a Turnpike Road. Marsden Lane was a well-developed track, possibly dating from Roman times if not even earlier.

There was almost definitely a ford crossing the River Colne at or near the bottom of Peel Street which would have connected Marsden Lane with Argyle Street.

Wessen Court was built on the site once occupied by Planks.
Judi Thorpe 2013

The earliest reference we have of a bridge of any kind dates from 1569 when the Almondbury Parish records include a report of a death by drowning dated 24.7.1569 when Jennet Marsden slipped from a bridge. Its location is not identified but it must have been located within the Marsden-in-Almondbury parish boundary and, thus, lie south of the River Colne. The bridge in question would almost definitely have been of wooden construction. It is tempting to think that it might have been where Towngate Bridge now stands. The sad report tells us that,

> **"Jennet ye wyffe off John Marsden by sodden chanche the 22 day off Julye slipped off a brigge as she was bowne to mylke or as she comed from the pasture the water beying up by reason off rayne that nyght and in the mornynge and was drowned and founde agayne about one off the clocke and was buried the 24 off Julye."**

The earliest Turnpike route through Marsden was in use from the early 1760s. It roughly follows an even earlier path leading from Marsden to Huddersfield and beyond. It is clearly marked by

Jefferys on his map of 1770 as taking a route approximating to the present day Meltham Road, Brougham Road and Market Place. It is shown as crossing the Wessenden Brook and turning into Towngate before continuing up Old Mount Road.

Jefferys does not mark a bridge over the Wessenden Brook but the strong, uninterrupted drawing of this road suggests that there was one on this site.

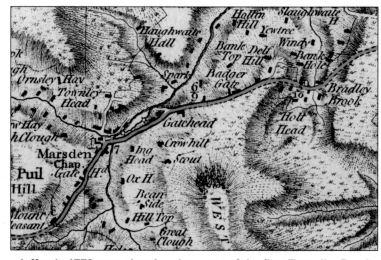

Jeffrey's 1770 map showing the route of the first Turnpike Road

Development of the Village Centre

**This is the only known image of Kaye's Bridge crossing the Wessenden Brook
which was replaced by the present bridge in 1876.
Marsden Photographic Archive**

An old stone bridge, known as Kaye's Bridge which connected Towngate with Market Place, stood on the site of the present Towngate Bridge at Bridge End. Whitehead states that this bridge was built in 1798 but all indications are that a bridge was in existence from a much earlier date. A document in the West Yorkshire Archive supports this. On the 4th July 1664 the inhabitants of Marsden presented a petition to '*The Honorable Justices of the Peace*' at the Quarter Sessions in Wakefield. Marsden had been assessed to pay towards the cost of repairing '*a wooden bridge over the river in Marsden*'. However the petitioners felt that their contribution was out of proportion to that of '*other neighbouring towns*'. They pointed out that the bridge in question was built before any of them could remember and they had no idea what the original repair arrangements were. They were clearly reluctant to take on the responsibility for something that a previous generation had undertaken. Unfortunately we do not know if they were successful but the record confirms the presence of a bridge which the petition states was used by people travelling to Lancashire and Cheshire. It is most probable that this wooden bridge was the forerunner to Towngate Bridge.

In 1723, the incumbent, Isaac Walton together with a Churchwarden, James Haigh who was the 'Constabble' and Mr. Mowbray the Surveyor along with 13 other signatories petitioned the Honourable Court for a payment of £21.7.6d. to meet the debt that they had incurred in building a bridge of '*sufficient stone*' and which they had no way of repaying. The bridge was erected in 1721 within the parish of Almondbury which indicates that it lay south of the River Colne and it seems likely that it lay on or near, the site of the present Towngate Bridge and was used to convey the first Turnpike over the Wessenden Brook. We have no record of whether their petition was successful or from whom they borrowed the money but one can only applaud their initiative.

Development of the Village Centre

There are later references to other footbridges. In addition to the one mentioned previously, connecting Station Road with Wessen Court, there was also Joe Grime Brig, a wooden footbridge, which crossed the Wessenden Brook between the White Hart and the existing house above, joining Towngate with Weirside.

Joe Grime was a coal merchant in the mid 1850s and would lend customers a hand-cart to wheel their coal home. When the bridge needed repair the council suggested that, as it only benefited the people using Fall Lane, they should repair it at their own cost. This laissez-faire approach was not uncommon in the affairs of the Marsden Council. The positions of these two bridges are integral to the properties in the oldest part of Marsden village centre namely Planks and Towngate.

Joe Grime Brig can be seen crossing the Wessenden Brook between 15 & 17 Towngate.
Marsden Photographic Archive

Development of the Village Centre

Jefferys shows two mills in the Brougham Road area. The mill nearest to the centre of the village was almost definitely The Corn Mill which would have been used by the inhabitants of the township to grind oats and other grains for their own use. The other mill is a very early textile mill.

The Canal Company map, probably produced in 1793, showed the route of the proposed canal and the position of the mills likely to be affected. The Old Corn Mill, the Factory and Upper End Mill are shown as belonging to Haigh. In addition to Haigh's mills the map also shows Clough Lea Mill, Middle Mill, Ottiwells Mill, Fall Lane Mill and Woodbottom Mill. These are highlighted on the map. The Canal Company's map, although not very accurately surveyed, also shows Towngate as being developed on both sides of the road all down its length and buildings spilling out into Market Place.

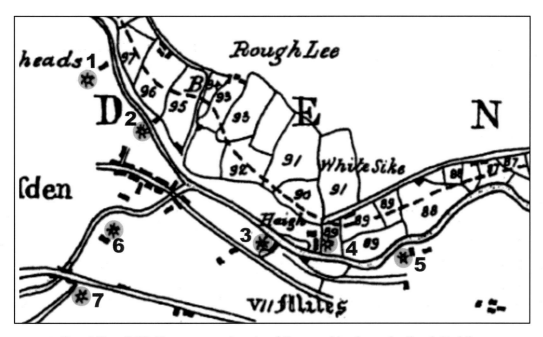

Canal Map 1793. The proposed route of the canal is shown by the dotted line.
Ref. QDP6 (CALS)

1. Clough Lee Mill	2. Middle Mill	3. The Old Corn Mill	4. Silk Mill and Upper End Mill
5. Wood Bottom Mill	6. Fall Lane Mill	7. Ottiwells Mill	

Tommy Mellor's Bridge is not shown on the 1793 map although it is believed to have existed for some long time before this date. Tommy Mellor, after whom the bridge is named, died in 1787.

Tommy Mellor's Bridge links The Green with Clough Lea.
Judi Thorpe 2013

Development of the Village Centre

The eastward extension of Pinfold Lane was known as Buckley Hill, the name being changed to Warehouse Hill with the arrival of the canal warehouse at the top.

Both the canal warehouse with its mortuary above and the attached wharfinger's cottage are shown on the Township map.

The Swan and adjacent cottages are also shown on the Township map. This area at the bottom of Peel Street was known as Cocklip, most probably referring to a place where the river was forded before a bridge was built, a 'cock leap'.

The rear of the canal warehouse and keeper's cottage alongside the canal, now converted to two dwellings.
Judi Thorpe 2013

The end of the 18th century marked the beginnings of an important change in the nature and size of Marsden.

The establishment of the early mills, although initially small enterprises, provided employment opportunities that, for the first time, were based outside the homes of the populace. This change was accompanied by a slow but significant increase in the population.

The Swan acquired a new frontage after Bentley and Shaw bought the property in 1926.
Judi Thorpe 2013

Clearly this growth in numbers of people presented a need for more housing and other amenities.

Houses, workshops and small shops selling foodstuffs extended beyond the core of the village and spread out to include Weirside, Argyle Street, Oliver Lane, the bottom of Peel Street on the western side and Market Place. Enoch Taylor established his blacksmith's shop in Goodall's Yard off Brougham Road, then still called Idle Row, near to a public house called the George and Dragon. Greenwood produced a map at the beginning of the 19th century which indicates this growth.

This map appears to be reasonably well surveyed and, although it lacks details of much that has been described above, it clearly shows that significant developments had taken place in Marsden during the 50 years since Jefferys' map was published.

Development of the Village Centre

Detail from Greenwood's map, surveyed between 1817 and 1818 showing the development of the village and the elaborate system of trackways connecting the outlying parts of Marsden to the centre of the village.

Greenwood's map shows three major additions to the infrastructure of the village; the bridging of the River Colne at the bottom of Peel Street, the Huddersfield to Ashton canal and the second Turnpike route which bypassed the Towngate area and ran along Carrs Road. These improvements in access into and out of Marsden were supported by Marsden people out of necessity due to the growing importance of the village as a centre of industry.

The canal was in use for traffic between Marsden and Huddersfield even before the Standedge Tunnel was completed and was finally opened throughout its length in 1811. According to a contemporary advertisement in the Huddersfield Examiner, goods were *'conveyed by the Huddersfield Canal Company from the Wharfe at Marsden daily to all parts'*. Most importantly the canal allowed easy bulk transportation of coal into the village to power the mill boilers.

Snailhorn Bridge, at the bottom of Peel Street, was built in 1798 at a cost of £90. It provided access for wheeled traffic travelling from the village centre via Argyle Street and was aligned with Warehouse Hill so as to provide easy vehicular access to the loading wharf on the canal. There was a crossing point at the bottom of Peel Street, prior to a bridge being built, made possible by the nature of the river bed at or near this point.

An engraving of Snailhorn Bridge, built in 1798, looking upstream.
Planks is on the left and the Swan cottages are on the right.
'William Schofield, An Earnest Yorkshire Methodist' 1882

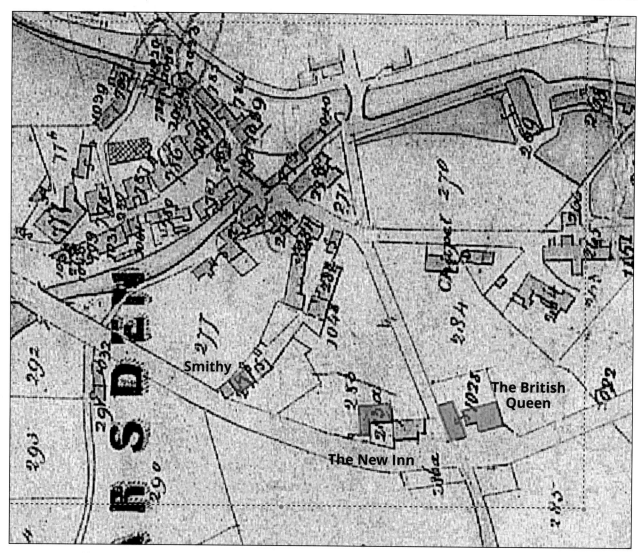

1848 Marsden-in-Almondbury Tithe Map showing the development of the village centre.
The British Queen, The New Inn and the Smithy have been highlighted.

The rerouting of the Turnpike along Carrs Road provided further impetus for the village to develop beyond the older centre around the church in Towngate. However, the 1848 Marsden-in-Almondbury Tithe Map clearly shows that the old centre is still significant in the life of the village.

Towngate is shown as having buildings on both sides of the road along its entire length although Peel Street remains almost undeveloped. The 1848 Tithe Map shows Oliver Lane, which runs from Market Place to Manchester Road, as having been developed for housing, some of which is still present today. There was a smithy at the far end near to the steps which lead up to Manchester Road. Traces of this building are still present in the wall on the right hand side.

Manchester Road, the A62, was completed in 1839. The Tithe Map shows the two hostelries which were built on each corner of Peel Street and Manchester Road to serve travellers; the British Queen which is now a private residence called Ingfield House and, on the opposite corner, the New Inn, which remains licensed to this day. Church Lane is marked, running from Towngate, around the old church and joining with Clough Lea. There are properties along its western side. Argyle Street, then called Thimble Street has properties along its length and The Red Lion is shown in Market Place.

Development of the Village Centre

The top of Oliver Lane c1900 with an old smithy on the right-hand side near to the steps leading up to Manchester Road.
Marsden Photographic Archive

The remains of the old smithy can be seen in the wall enclosing the garden of the large house at the top of Oliver Lane.
Judi Thorpe 2013

The population of Marsden hovered around the 2,000 mark for the first 40 years of the 19th century. However, there was a massive growth in the industrialisation of textile production from the 1850s onwards. This led to workers moving into the village, attracted by the availability of employment opportunities. By 1851 the population of the village was recorded as being 2,665 and the 1921 census showed that this number had increased dramatically to reach a peak of 5,962.

Population

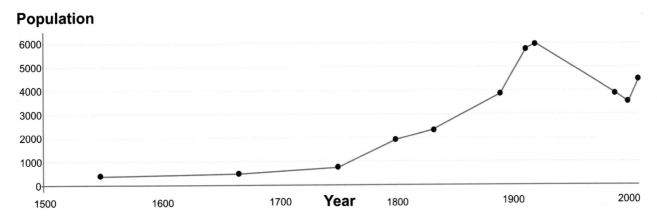

The population of Marsden from 1500 to 2010

As the industrialisation of textile production grew it continued to further impact on the lives of the people of the village in that there was a gradual, but growing, shift from home-based work to factory-based employment. The lives of women, in particular, began to change from the traditional work of running a home to working for wages. The 1851 census highlights this change in the economy. The list of occupations shown in the census includes, dressmakers, tailors, milliners, clog makers, butchers, bakers and grocers carrying out their businesses from their own establishments around the village. There was an increasing number of joiners, blacksmiths and stonemasons. In addition to the availability of goods and services the village also required the provision of education, places of worship and for the supply of houses to keep pace with need.

Development of the Village Centre

Education

The first purpose-built school, the Town School, was built in 1820 on Idle Row. It was built by public subscription and largely supported by the nonconformist leaders of the community, amongst whom was Enoch Taylor, the Marsden iron founder. In response to growing numbers, the school was replaced by a larger building on the same site in 1878.

This school building was enlarged in 1902 following complaints from school inspectors about the inadequacy of the accommodation. Cllr. Firth, a school governor, had reported the previous year that, although they had seating for 183 children in the mixed department, there were actually 276 children on the register. The building remains to this day, with later additions, as the Nursery and Infant School. A Wesleyan Chapel was built soon after 1820 next to the original school and master's house. The building was demolished in 1968 and the land purchased by the council to allow space for the school to expand once more.

Marsden Nursery and Infants School on Brougham Road built on the site of the first Town School.
Judi Thorpe 2013

Idle Row was renamed Brougham Road in 1863 at the suggestion of John Bower Robinson who felt it more appropriate because, with its Wesleyan Chapel and schools, the road was *'no longer occupied by ne'er-do-wells'*. Although this makes a good story, the name Idle Row probably comes not from a description of the habits of its occupants, but from the old dialect use of 'idle' to mean a small stream. Such a stream, now almost entirely culverted, runs past one end of the old houses on the southern side of the road opposite New Mills. Lord Brougham was a politician and lawyer who defended the Luddites when they were tried in 1813 for the murder of William Horsfall in 1812.

The Church built its first school in 1829 on the corner of Church Lane and Clough Lea. Government grants allowed the church to build another school for older children in 1855. The site chosen was behind the cottages that we now call Throstle Nest on the corner of Old Mount Road and Manchester Road. At the opening ceremony the Rev. Charles Hulbert of Slaithwaite said he could not help but compare the building to Westminster Hall. The building continued to be used as a school until it was demolished in 1967.

The National School, built in 1855 with the first Master, Alfred Hirst, and his wife.
Marsden Photographic Archive

Development of the Village Centre

The West Riding County Council assumed responsibility for education in 1902 and built the 'Council School' on Manchester Road. The opening of the building which was said to be *'bright, well-equipped and arranged on the most modern lines for the accommodation of 420 mixed scholars'* was reported in the 22nd July, 1910 edition of the Colne Valley Guardian. Since 1960 it has housed the Junior School age children of the village.

The schools referred to here were built between 1820 and 1910. However, out of economic necessity, children left school as soon as the law allowed them to.

The school-leaving age was raised to 12 years in 1899 and the opportunity to continue learning was provided by Sunday schools and evening classes.

Marsden Council School, built on Manchester Road in 1910, now houses the Junior School.
Marsden Photographic Archive

The Mechanics' Institute was built entirely by public subscription in 1861. It provided for the self-improvement and social needs of the village. The hall on the first floor was in constant use for dances, concerts and meetings.

The ground floor provided meeting rooms and a library which appears to have been well used despite the fact that patrons were not allowed to take books off the shelves themselves but had to ask a librarian. For many years the nursery classes of the Town School were housed in part of the building. William Henry Firth, a Marsden mill owner, left a legacy for the erection of a stone clock tower, however, the building was not able to support such a structure. A wooden tower designed by James Kirk & Son was, therefore, substituted. The clock was manufactured by William Potts of Leeds.

Fred Russell's Newsagent and Stationery shop can be seen in this photograph on the right hand side of Market Place. He was a prolific photographer of village life.

Marsden Mechanics' Institute.
Marsden Photographic Archive

Development of the Village Centre

Religious Life

The Anglican community of Marsden worshipped in the Towngate churches which we described at the beginnning of this chapter. However, from the beginning of the 19th century, there was also a growth in nonconformism. The first active group of Marsden nonconformists initially met in a cottage on the Green in 1790. They built their first church on Buckley Hill, at the bottom of Peel Street, in 1807 and continue to this day to call the building The Green Chapel in reference to its early beginnings. This building was demolished and the site redeveloped with a new church in 1858.

The Sunday school bears a stone dated 1890. It was laid by Mrs. Joseph Crowther in celebration of the centenary of the Congregational Church. This building was converted into flats in 2007

The Congregational Church, built in 1807, was the first nonconformist church in the village. The History of Marsden Congregational Church 1900.

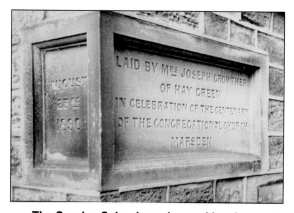

The Sunday School was housed in a large building at the side of the church. The foundation stone remains. Judi Thorpe 2012

The first Wesleyan Methodist Chapel was built alongside the Town School on Brougham Road in 1824. This single storey chapel was replaced by a larger building in 1871 and continued as the home of Methodism in Marsden until falling congregations necessitated its closure in the late 1960s.

With the closure of the Wesleyan Methodist Chapel the Methodists joined the Congregationalists in 1968 at their church to form The United Church. The present church was built in 1931 on the same site. The graveyard was closed in 1855 and the area was later used for car parking.

The Wesleyan Chapel built in 1871 between the Town School and the Mechanics' Institute on Brougham Road. 'William Schofield, An Earnest Yorkshire Methodist' pub 1882

Development of the Village Centre

**The Congregational Church, otherwise known as The Green Chapel,
c1900 before the present church was built in 1931.
Marsden Photographic Archive**

**The church is now called the United Church Marsden.
Judi Thorpe 2013**

Development of the Village Centre

Housing

As the need arose, mill-owners and speculative builders responded by building houses. Terrace housing, often back-to-back, was built along Brougham Road. Derby Terrace, for example, which is opposite the Nursery and Infant School, was built in 1877.

A comparison of a plan of part of the village centre produced for an auction of property in the 1870s and the 1895 O.S. map demonstrates very clearly the changes that took place during a period of 35 years on the land to the east of the Wessenden Brook. The plan also shows Peel Street and Argyle Street with their earlier names of Ready Carr Road and Thimble Street. Thimble Street was, in the very early days, part of the main route through the village centre. Tracks from the east on both sides of the River Colne converged near to the bottom end of Thimble Street. Having journeyed up the street, travellers then either continued up Weirside and Fall Lane to reach Wessenden Head and the settlements scattered around Binn, or, turned right over the Wessenden Brook into Towngate and beyond. As Brougham Road developed into the main road so Argyle Street became merely a short road of houses and shops.

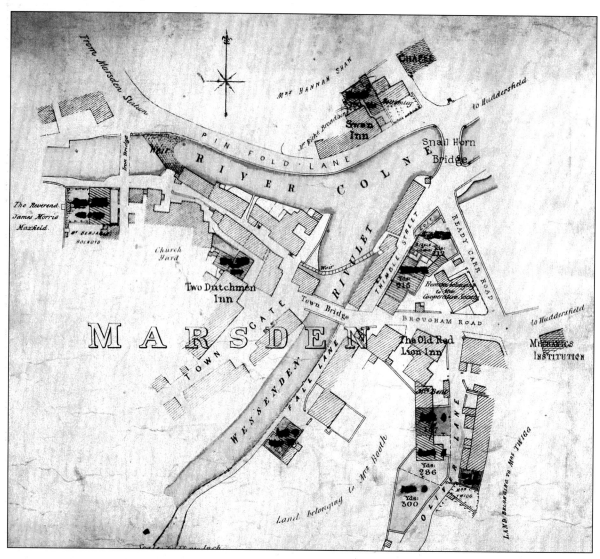

1870s plan of property to be auctioned in the centre of Marsden.
Weirside, marked as Fall Lane, was narrower than it is now, particularly towards the south.
West Yorkshire Archive

Development of the Village Centre

Perhaps the most notable occupant of Thimble Street was the Rev. James Bond who, on his retirement in 1846 as the minister of the Congregationalist Church, ran a small school in one of the cottages.

At the Peel Street end of the street a lady called Bathsheba Garside kept a butcher's shop and a slaughter house. This building, at the time of the demolition of the properties on the river side in 1974, was Duncan's barber's shop.

Argyle Street was once a main road connecting Towngate with the routes to the south and east of the village.
Marsden Photographic Archive

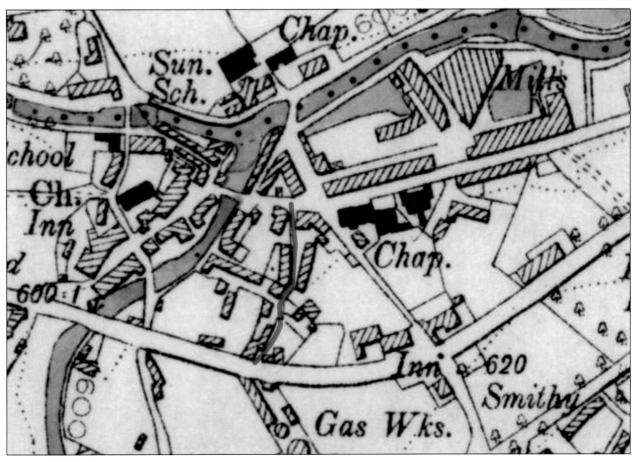

The 1895 O.S. map shows the in-fill housing on Oliver Lane, highlighted in red, opposite the pre-existing older cottages.

Development of the Village Centre

Plans for proposed building development had to be passed by the council but, as in the present day, things did not always go smoothly. An article in the Slaithwaite and Colne Valley News dated 19th August, 1898 reported an incident of some few years previously. Joseph Pinder, owner of Pinder's Yard, (now called Garfield Place) obtained permission for the erection of some houses at the top of Oliver Lane.

However, *'the owner took it upon himself powers which the law had conferred on the council. That is to say, a stone wall was erected in front of the houses and setts put down, the result of which was to throw the road out of proper line'.* The council surveyor, *'at the head of an army of six stalwart workmen'* was dispatched to demolish the offending wall. An altercation took place which involved Joe Pinder brandishing *'a huge fine old English cavalry sabre'*, whereupon the workforce withdrew feeling that their wages of 41/2d. an hour did not justify risking their lives. A second onslaught was mounted at 4.00am on the following Saturday morning when *'five able-bodied men under the leadership of the council's shrewd surveyor and escorted by three stalwart guardians of the peace and property marched'* along Oliver Lane. Joe Pinder was, apparently, asleep throughout this second, successful, attempt to demolish the wall.

The rapid expansion of house building continued apace into the first half of the 1900s. In 1902 contracts were awarded to the Co-op to build 36 cottages above Marsden Lane at Grange. The Huddersfield Examiner dated 15th March, 1902 reported that, *'This addition to the number of houses for the workpeople of Marsden will meet a long felt want as so many persons come daily by train from the neighbouring villages to work in Marsden'.*

An auction sale of property and land in the Station Road area was advertised in the Huddersfield Examiner dated 25th June, 1904. The six houses which formed Shaw's Terrace, the dwelling house and farm buildings known as Utlock, together with Godfrey Close divided into four lots were sold. The advertisement stated that the land and properties were situated *'near to the railway station and in one of the best positions in Marsden. The land is admirably adapted for building purposes and is almost the only available building land near the centre of the town'.* Shaw's Terrace and Utlock are still present and the houses on the eastern side of Station Road were built although some of the land remained undeveloped and is now used for allotments behind the Conservative Club. The houses on the western side of Station Road followed soon afterwards.

The shortage of building land in the centre of Marsden led to housing developments spreading out along and above Marsden Lane, Manchester Road, Brougham Road, Carrs Road and Mount Road.

The 1908 O.S. map shows much of this development although the houses which were built on Station Road and along Victoria Street, which was built at the bottom of what was Godfrey Close, were not present when this map was surveyed. House building continued to be necessary and in 1911 the Co-op built another 54 houses at Lower Plains.

Development of the Village Centre

Shopping

Many of the houses in Towngate, Church Lane, Argyle Street, Bridge End, Market Place and Buckley Hill used a room fronting onto the street as a shop selling a limited range of groceries, meat, home-baked bread and oatcakes. These premises became inadequate as the demands for more goods and services grew which led to the development of purpose-built commercial properties in Peel Street.

The 1908 O.S. map also shows the shift from Towngate to Peel Street as the main centre of village retail activity.

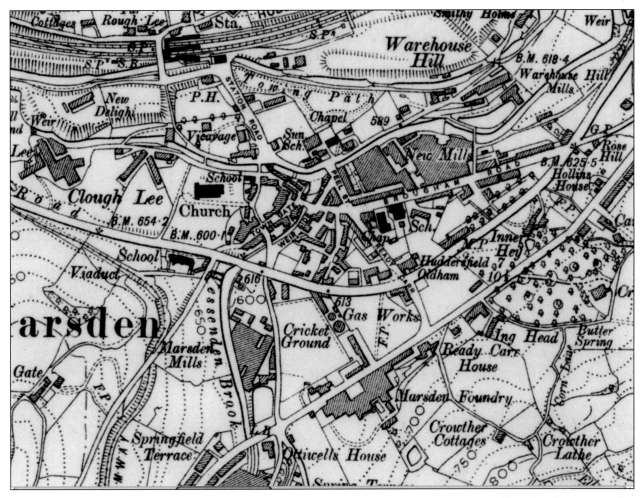

1908 O.S. Map showing the spread of housing and purpose-built shops throughout the village in response to the influx of workers needed to staff the larger and more numerous mills.

Development of the Village Centre

The lower section of Ready Carr Road was renamed Peel Street when, in the late 1800s, this area was developed along both sides to provide shops with living accommodation above.

The eastern side of lower Peel Street was developed at the very end of the 1800s and seen here some 40 years later.
Marsden Photographic Archive

William Johnstone, a Scot, established a grocery business in 1835 at Bridge End, so called because the site was adjacent to Towngate Bridge.

William Johnstone's first shop is the property on the far side of Towngate Bridge with a gas light attached.
Marsden Photographic Archive

His trade developed to such an extent that he was able to build an emporium to house his expanded range of goods to include drapery, coal, corn and a Post Office. Johnstone's business was housed in the imposing building at the bottom of Peel Street which still stands today.

At some time Johnstone divided the property and Lloyds Bank occupied part of the building. The grocery business closed in the late 1970s and, after several short-lived enterprises, opened as The Riverhead Brewery and Tap. The former bank now bears the appropriate name of The Wine Bank.

William Johnstone's emporium at the bottom of Peel Street.
Marsden Photographic Archive

Development of the Village Centre

The development of purpose-built shops continued on the western side of the top section of Peel Street between Market Place and Manchester Road to provide a continuous shopping street. These properties are still trading as retail businesses. The old Shakespeare Inn stood on the cobbled area above the Mechanics' Institute. This was demolished and the new Shakespeare Inn with two adjacent shops, now housing a fish and chip shop and florist's were built in 1923.

It is possible that Johnstone's trade was adversely affected by the formation of the Co-op. In the mid 1800s The Marsden Self-Help Co-operative Society began life in a small shop adjacent to the Congregational Church. The business prospered and, several years later, acquired premises at the corner of Peel Street and Market Place.

The first Co-op began in very small premises adjacent to the Congregational Church.
Marsden Photographic Archive

The second Co-op shop occupied the site of the present, much grander, building.
Marsden Photographic Archive

The shop buildings on both corners of lower Peel Street were built and occupied by the Co-op from 1896.
Marsden Photographic Archive

Development of the Village Centre

This property was demolished and replaced in 1896 on the same site by the larger Marsden Equitable Industrial Society shop which continues to prosper. The Co-op also built the shops on the opposite side of Peel Street which now house Mozzarella's Bistro. In addition to their main store there were branches on Binn Road, Smithy Holme on Marsden Lane and Lingard's Terrace on Manchester Road.

The Co-op was obviously an enterprising organisation with many projects developing over time, for example, on 9th December, 1911 the Marsden Council Meeting received plans from the Co-op for the erection of a tripery, sausage room and stables at Warehouse Hill. Before the invention of motorised transport all bulk goods were carried by horse and cart. These premises have now been converted to houses and named Cavendish Court.

Development of the Village Centre

Market Place

The name Market Place is a puzzle. It is certainly in a central position to the village but old photographs and newspaper reports indicate that markets and fairs were actually held in Towngate. It is possible that Market Place may have been the original site of a market but that the sheer size of livestock sales made the site impractical. White's Directory published in 1853 lists the three fairs held annually in Marsden as being 25th April, 1853, 11th July, 1853 and 25th September, 1853. Cattle, pigs and sheep were herded into the village to be sold.

The Huddersfield Examiner dated 26th September, 1863 reported that hundreds of sheep were put up for sale and that they *'seemed possessed of a wayward and refractory temper'*. On 26th April, 1902 the Huddersfield Examiner criticised the *'custom of holding the fair in the busiest street and thus blocking up the places of business'*. Furthermore the evidence of the presence of so many animals *'deserved the attention of the local sanitary inspector'*.

Market Place extends from Bridge End to Peel Street, a very short distance. It was also a narrow road with the Red Lion, built in 1787, dominating the centre. The 1838 valuation of this old coaching inn described it as a substantial property covering a quarter of an acre with stables and outbuildings. This land lay behind the inn to the western side of Oliver Lane and extended over the area now occupied by the early 1900s housing development in Market Walk. In 1911 it was proposed that the building should be demolished so as to allow Market Place to be widened.

The Old Red Lion before the new frontage was built in order to widen Market Place.
Marsden Photographic Archive

A compromise was reached in which the frontage was removed and replaced with the present one. This allowed the new frontage to the property to line up with the shops on either side. The building is now used as a solicitor's office with flats above. The present day butcher's shop and the hairdresser's, to the right of the public house were built in 1904 to replace older properties. The two shops on the left of the Old Red Lion were built as part of the upper Peel Street development. The opposite side of Market Place is largely occupied by the Co-op.

This photograph was taken facing Towngate Bridge and shows Market Place as it was in the 1920s.
Marsden Photographic Archive

Development of the Village Centre

Weirside/Fall Lane Bottom

The road that we now call Weirside runs alongside the Wessenden Brook from Towngate Bridge up to the tunnel under Manchester Road. At that point its name changes to Fall Lane as it continues up the hill to the roundabout at Ottiwells. However, the whole road from Towngate Bridge to Ottiwells was originally called Fall Lane. The building on the corner of Weirside and Bridge End, next to Knight's butcher's shop, was originally built as a shop with living accommodation above. It has now been converted to exclusively residential use.

Attached to this property is an imposing residence called Argyle House which was built on the foundations of two cottages which had previously occupied the site. Weirside was a narrow back lane when these two properties were built. This can easily be recognised by the fact that the front door to Argyle House faces onto Market Walk which, at the time it was built, was still undeveloped open land. It is apparent that, from the door and windows on the property which face onto Wessenden Brook, the level of Weirside has been raised. This change of level possibly occurred sometime in the mid 1700s and was perhaps associated with the building of the weir across the Wessenden Brook. The original level of Weirside can be identified by the change in the masonry of the wall enclosing the Wessenden Brook.

The rear of Argyle House showing that the level of Weirside has been raised.
Judi Thorpe 2013

A proposal was made by the Marsden Local Board to replace Kaye's Bridge (Towngate Bridge) with an iron one, to widen Fall lane and to create a new bridge (Taylor's Bridge) over the Wessenden Brook to join Fall Lane with Towngate. A Government Inquiry was held in Marsden on the 24th of January 1875 and the plans were accepted. The work was completed in 1876.

Fall Hall adjoins Argyle House and, similarly, has its original front door facing onto Market Walk. It was built some time not later than the mid-1800s after the road level had been altered. The next old property up the road towards the tunnel is now a house called The Old Barn present in 1793. However, up to 40 years ago, it was the slaughterhouse used by the Waterhouse's and, later, Knight's butcher's shop in Market Place.

Fall Hall was also an important house with its frontage facing onto what is now an area of high density 19th century housing.
Judi Thorpe 2013

Development of the Village Centre

The buildings at the top of Weirside included small shops and, next to the tunnel, a cinema built in 1918 by a travelling showman, Tommy Leyland, who settled in Marsden.

The building had a corrugated tin roof which proved to be very noisy when there was heavy rain. This did not seriously detract from the enjoyment of patrons when movies were silent but interfered considerably following the invention of talkies.

Sadly the Electric Theatre closed in 1975. It was demolished when a fall of snow brought the roof down. The site was developed with the new houses present today.

Taylor's Bridge was built in 1875 to link Weirside with Towngate and Church Lane. An early photograph showing the properties on Towngate, taken from Weirside, shows the house that was demolished to make way for the bridge.

It is to the left of the small building, The Old Cobblers, which is still present and now stands on the approach to the bridge.

This 1930s image, looking down Weirside towards Market Place, shows a lock-up shop at the bottom right followed by the end of Garfield Place, the old slaughter house, Fall Hall and Argyle House.
Marsden Photographic Archive

This photograph, taken from Taylor's Bridge, shows the terrace of four houses occupying the site of the cinema and the lock-up shop.
Judi Thorpe 2013

This very early photograph, taken from Weirside, shows the continuous line of buildings on the eastern side of Towngate.
Marsden Photographic Archive

Development of the Village Centre

The intention was to build the bridge to provide a direct link onto Church Lane. However there were difficulties because Towngate was at a lower level to that of Weirside which had been raised at an earlier date. Thus the level of the road in Towngate had to be raised.

The old cobblers and the house opposite, No. 19 Towngate, were both affected. The original level of the land is particularly apparent in the back yard of No. 19. A flight of steps now provide access to the kitchen door which was originally at ground floor level. The present building was erected at a later date on the foundations of the old house. On the Towngate side of the bridge a relic of the original cobbled road surface remains immediately in front of No. 17.

Church Lane was an ancient and narrow trackway which had been adequate for pedestrians and handcarts. However once the road started to carry heavier traffic problems arose.

There was already a bridge, Union Bridge, crossing the River Colne at the far end of Church Lane. Whitehead states that this bridge had been built some 14 years before Taylor's Bridge in 1861. He also says that there was previously a set of stepping stones to ford the river on the site.

Church Lane, leading up to the railway station, was inadequate for the traffic it had to carry being only 7' wide in places.
Marsden Photographic Archive

The bridge was given the name Union Bridge in 1888 because it united the parishes of Marsden-in-Huddersfield which lay north of the River Colne with Marsden-in-Almondbury to the south. The reasons for building the bridge are not known but it can be supposed that access to the railway station coupled with plans to build a bridge to link Weirside with Church Lane influenced the project.

This photograph shows the bridge to have been a single span, iron girder bridge. It was of similar design to the present Taylor's and Towngate bridges and it is virtually certain that it was also made by the Marsden Iron Foundry.

Union Bridge united the two Marsden parishes.
Marsden Photographic Archive

Development of the Village Centre

Church Lane

The provision of the two bridges at either end of Church Lane gave a direct route to the railway station from the foundry on Carrs Road and the mills in the Wessenden valley. Taylor's Iron Foundry certainly used the railway to transport goods such as the large and very heavy steam boilers.

Perhaps prompted by the complaints made by the railway company that their vehicles were getting damaged by being scraped along the walls enclosing Church Lane, a petition was made in 1886 by some of the inhabitants of the village which pointed out that Church Lane was '*one of the principal thoroughfares of the village*' and urgently needed to be widened. The Slaithwaite Guardian of September 1887 reported that, '*The widening of Church Lane became a burning question*'.

All agreed that the road should be widened but it proved impossible to find a solution as to how this could be achieved. The village was split between those who wanted the properties on the western side of the road to be demolished and those who proposed that the old churchyard should be narrowed necessitating the removal of bodies.

The question of Church Lane went on smouldering for a further ten years when another attempt was made to reach a solution. In 1897 a new proposal was made but was rejected in a ballot of ratepayers. The project was left for another 14 years when, in 1911, it was raised once more and, once more, rejected by the ratepayers. However, all was not lost. Plans drawn up by the council in 1924 were approved – a mere 41 years after the problem was first identified.

Church Lane was finally widened in 1928 following 41 years of discussion.
Marsden Photographic Archive

The solution involved the demolition of the properties on the western side of Church Lane and a narrow strip of land being taken from the perimeter of the old graveyard. The church community agreed strongly that the aspect of the new church would be greatly improved by the removal of the old properties that stood in front of it.

Development of the Village Centre

In addition, the old church school, which stood on the corner of Church Lane and Clough Lea, had ceased to be used as a school in 1910. Following its closure the building was used as a church hall but became redundant with the offer from John Edward Crowther to provide a new Parochial Church Hall. This was built in Clough Lea in 1925. In addition the old church had been demolished, thus removing an obstacle, and a promise that bodies would be removed to the new churchyard with due respect was made. Finally everyone was reassured that the best solution had been arrived at. The splendidly wide Church Lane was finally finished in 1928. The original Union Bridge was replaced by a much wider concrete structure as part of the scheme. This was itself replaced by the present bridge in 2009/10 with a fish ladder running under the bridge in the centre of the old weir.

The improvement of the roads in the village was not welcomed by everyone. In 1908 Cllr Hoyle *'drew attention to the excessive speed at which a person connected with repair works at Butterley was accustomed to ride through the village on a motor bicycle. It was a positive danger as the man went like a flash something like 15 – 20 miles an hour'.* He possibly still rued the day in 1896 when legislation raised the speed limit from 4mph to 14mph and the abolition of the requirement that *'horseless carriages'* be preceded by a pedestrian waving a red flag.

Development of the Village Centre

Manchester Road

The third turnpike route was completed in 1839 and created what we now call the A62, Manchester Road. Manchester Road separates the present day village centre from that part of Marsden which lies above, to the south.

Manchester Road in 1913, when this photograph was taken, carried considerably less traffic than it does today. The park seen on the right had recently been opened. Marsden Photographic Archive

The earliest development to take place on the 1839 turnpike was the two coaching inns, The New Inn and the British Queen, on each side of the junction of Manchester Road with Peel Street. The New Inn remains as a hostelry but the British Queen is now a private residence called Ingfield House.

The New Inn was built to cater for travellers using the new turnpike which ran along the route of the present day A62. 'Marsden Memories' published in 1979 by the Marsden Festival Committee

Development of the Village Centre

Over the years, housing and other properties were built along both sides of Manchester Road. To the west of the New Inn, Leathholm Royd was built in 1904. On the opposite side of the road are the old Fire Station, built in 1909, and the attached Ambulance Station, built in 1914.

The buildings are now in the process of being converted to other uses. Until very recently the Fire Station was housed nearby in a converted petrol station. Despite protestations from the local community, it closed at midnight on May 2nd 2013.

The Gas Works, opened in 1856, stood to the side of the old fire station. At the time it was opened seven of the village mills, the Foundry, the new National School and some private buildings were fitted and ready to be connected to the gas supply. The gas holder remained long after the gas works closed and was only demolished in the 1970s.

The Fire and Ambulance Stations built in 1909 and 1914 respectively are awaiting redevelopment.
Judi Thorpe 2012

To the east of Ingfield House, terrace housing, such as Park View and Sunny Lea, built in 1910, was erected. Sherbrook cottages are older, probably dating from the 1830s.

Sherbrook cottages, were near to the tram terminus and housed the Tramway Parcel Depot.
Park View is the terrace to the right.
Judi Thorpe 2013

Development of the Village Centre

The Park

**Marsden Park celebrated its centenary in 2012. After years of neglect it has been restored
by the hard work and enthusiasm of a group of committed volunteers.
Marsden Photographic Archive**

The Park was opened in 1912 to provide healthy exercise and amusement for residents and visitors alike. A book produced by the Friends of Marsden Park entitled 'The Marsden Park Centenary 1912-2012' provides a comprehensive history of this important amenity which still plays a role in the leisure time of the village. The book describes the park in 1936, '*The pretty little park near the tram terminus gives dignity and importance to Marsden, for it has proved a great boon … Tennis and bowls are available, and music is discoursed from the bandstand during the summer months.*'

To the east of Marsden Park is the Junior School, built by the council in 1910 in what had originally been part of the garden of Inner Hey, an imposing house which remains as a residence.

The Colne Valley Constituency Labour Party was established in 1891, two years before the formation of the Independent Labour Party (ILP) and eight years before the national Labour Party. Victor Grayson was elected as an ILP MP in 1907. The Socialist Club, opposite Inner Hey, was built in 1911, the foundation stone having been laid by him. There are two other political clubs in the village. The Conservative Club on Victoria Street was built in 1908 although the club was established in 1879 when the members met in one of the houses in Derby Terrace. In accordance with the fervid teetotalism of the day no intoxicating liquor was allowed to be sold on the premises. Fortunately this rule does not apply to the present club.

The Liberal Club on Peel Street was established in 1874 and enlarged in 1905.

Chapter 3 - New Mills and Lakeside

The site now occupied by New Mills lies between Brougham Road and the River Colne and between Peel Street and Bruce's End. This large mill complex in the middle of the village grew over time taking in and adapting or demolishing older mill premises which once stood in the area. The earliest building on the site was a corn mill. This may have been built by the Lord of the Manor for the use of villagers who, for a fee, would bring their crop to be ground into flour. It is not known when the Corn Mill was established but a document in the West Yorkshire Archive refers to an application made in 1560 for reparation *at the mill in Marsden*. The old corn mill building remained after John Dowse established his corn milling business at Hey Green around 1795. John Haigh bought the empty property and adapted it for use as a cotton mill. At the same time he bought Frank Mill which had been built on the site to the east of the old corn mill. He was made bankrupt when his extensive cotton manufacturing business failed and these two mills were sold at auction in 1809

Extract from The Leeds Mercury, 18th November, 1809.
MARSDEN MILLS, &c To be SOLD by AUCTION

At the George Inn in Huddersfield, on Tuesday The Twelfth Day of December, 1809, due to the Bankruptcy of Mr. John Haigh.

Lot 111. All that very valuable COTTON MILL, called New Mill 63' x 34', Three storeys high besides the Garrets, with the Reservoir, originally belonging to the same when occupied as a Corn Mill and a Plot or Parcel of Land extending from the South End of the said Mill across the Hawm Ing to the old Turnpike Road. The Mill is well supplied with Water and turned by a Water Wheel 16' Diameter by 11' 7" broad.

Lot 1V. All that small MILL called Frank's Mill 35' x 23', Three Storeys high, turned by a Water Wheel 30' in Diameter by 2' 3" broad with a reservoir belonging to the same.

In addition to the two mills described above, a third mill was erected on the site in the early 1800s.

These three mills are shown on the 1854 6" O.S. map.

Reading from left to right are the later New Mill, the Old Corn Mill and Frank Mill.

Detail of the 1854 O.S. map showing three mills in the village centre

New Mills and Lakeside

Each of the three mills had its own dam. Frank Mill dam was fed by a stream running down from Scout, through Inner Hey garden and into the River Colne although, as has been recorded, this was not always an adequate source of water. A contemporary description of Frank Mill just before it was demolished in 1901 states,'*The running as with all water wheel mills, was very uncertain and intermittent and enforced short time was frequent. In the summer months, when the somewhat large dam was run off, the machinery had to stand idle.*'

The mill at the extreme left, New Mill, was built at a later date and, perhaps because of an advance in technology, incorporated a complicated waterway system which enabled a constant supply of water to keep its dam topped up. The New Mill dam was supplied by a goit which ran from above the weir built across the River Colne by Union Bridge at the bottom of Station Road and through Planks. Another weir on the Wessenden Brook allowed the water to pass under Argyle Street (still called Thimble Street on the map below) and Peel Street before entering the New Mill dam. Both these weirs are still present. A map produced around 1870 in connection with an auction of properties in the centre of the village clearly shows the path of the goit. It is almost certain that the goit connecting the two rivers existed before the houses in Planks were built.

This map shows that the houses in one of the two alleyways which formed Planks are built on each side of the goit.

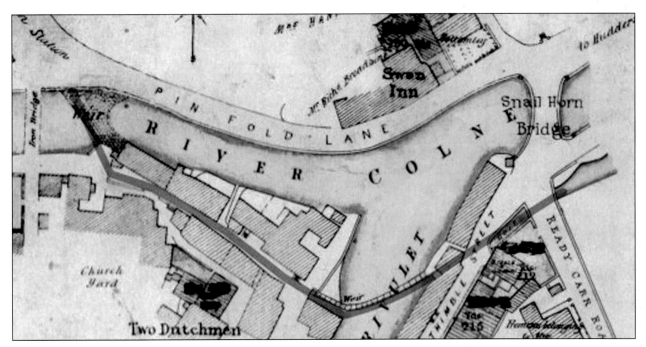

1870s plan of property to be auctioned in the centre of Marsden. The path of the goit is shown in blue.
WYAS, Kirklees KC391/85

New Mills and Lakeside

The stone paving slabs running down between the houses in Planks cover the goit which supplied water to the New Mill dam.
Marsden Photographic Archive

This photograph shows the route of the goit now covered with large stone paving slabs. Is it possible that the original covering was indeed timber planking which could explain the unusual name of this area of housing?

The photograph, below, dating from about 1870 shows what is now the Riverhead building on the corner of Argyle Street and Peel Street which, at the time this image was taken, was still undeveloped on its eastern side. The mill dam is clearly seen.

The track called Kiln Lane and later, Lodging House Lane which runs between the dam and the River Colne was once part of the main thoroughfare into the village from the Huddersfield direction. It followed a route from the White House public house above Slaithwaite, down Meltham Road to Gatehead and then dropped diagonally down to the River Colne before turning westwards to connect with Argyle Street. This pathway gradually went out of use as Brougham Road developed in importance to become the main road from the east into the centre of the village.

Photograph c1880, now on display in the Riverhead Tap

New Mills and Lakeside

Frank Mill was once owned by James Mellor, a shawl manufacturer. A photograph taken around 1895 shows purpose-built tenter frames stretching shawl fabric to size. Although not visible, the old mill dam still existed between the tenter posts and the River Colne. To the left of the Congregational Church were two cottages and The Swan, which are present today, although the public house was given a new frontage at a later date.

To the right of the church was a stable and the original Co-op shop, both properties are still present.

Snailhorn Bridge at the bottom of Lower Peel Street before the road was developed with shops on its eastern side in the late 1890s.
Marsden Photographic Archive

The photograph on the next page is a very good picture of the original Snailhorn Bridge, a three-arched stone bridge built in 1798/9 at Cocklip. It was built to enable wheeled traffic to pass from Argyle Street onto Warehouse Hill to reach the canal warehouse at the top. This gave the bridge a rather odd angle in relation to Peel Street which led to it resembling a snail shell and this is thought to be the reason for its name.

Prior to a bridge being built at this point the river was crossed using the flat stone river bed which is evident in the photograph. The newly built large mill in the picture indicates the growing importance of the textile trade and the attendant need to build more workers' houses. In response to this need Derby Terrace, the long row of houses on the top right, was built in 1877 by the mill owner to house his workers. The smaller mill building on the left is probably the original New Mill which was demolished in 1901 to make way for the further expansion of mill property.

Snailhorn Bridge c1880.
Marsden Photographic Archive

A postcard produced in around 1900 shows that the old mill is still present to the right of the larger mill building but the area formerly occupied by the mill dam and tenter posts is now covered by new weaving sheds.

Detail of postcard showing the expansion of mill buildings
on the New Mills site.
Marsden Photographic Archive

New Mills and Lakeside

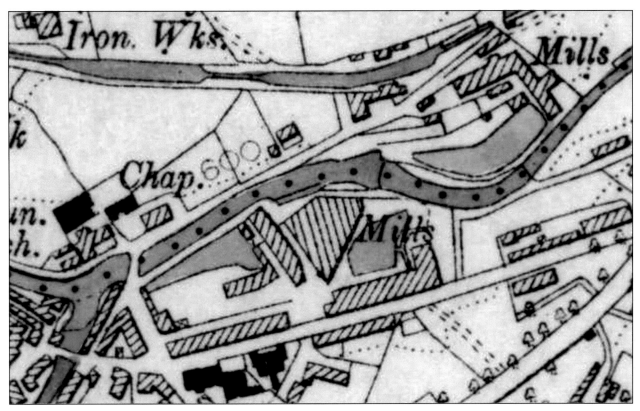

Detail of 1895 O.S. map

Although published in 1895, this map is based on an 1890 survey which explains why Snailhorn Bridge is shown in its original configuration even though it had been replaced by the present bridge in 1891. The decline of the canal as the principal means of conveying bulk goods occurred as the railway took precedence. This necessitated traffic having to turn left onto Station Road to reach the railway and its goods yard. The orientation of the old bridge made this difficult.

A large mill shed now occupies the site of the old Corn Mill and the middle of the three mill dams. A further mill building stretches out along Brougham Road with Derby Terrace to its left. Permission was granted in 1906 for the mill building to extend over the river. Kiln Lane is still evident running from Peel Street along the riverside although, by this time, it was no longer in use.

New Mills and Lakeside

The 1908 O.S. map, based on a 1904 revision, shows that the mill complex had developed as two blocks separated by a mill building.

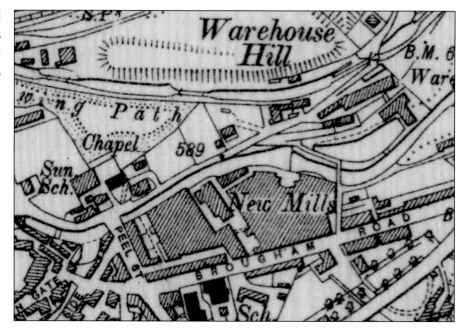

Detail of 1908 O.S.map

By 1949 the final expansion of New Mills had taken place and is shown on the map below as extending from Brougham Road across the river to the bottom of Warehouse Hill.

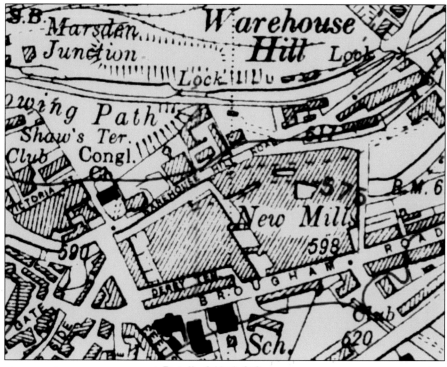

Detail of 1949 O.S. map

New Mills and Lakeside

This photograph shows the gable end of what is now called Frank Mill. It stands on Brougham Road at the south-east corner of the New Mills site and is an older building than those around it.

Although it is not in the same position as the original Frank Mill the name was retained, as was the name of the manufacturer who built it; the north-east corner of the site is still known as Bruce's End.

This building, although occupying a different site from the original, still retains the old name of Frank Mill.
Judi Thorpe 2012

This view of Marsden, taken from the top of the church tower in 1980, shows the full and final extent of New Mills with the shops of Peel Street in front of it and Warehouse Hill to its left. The mill chimney has been moved across the river to the north side. The mill is typical of those which flourished in the Colne Valley at the height of the woollen trade in the first half of the 20th century. The mill complex was part of the Crowther empire along with Bank Bottom, Ready Carr and Fall Lane Mills. The large development of new housing at the top right is the Woods Estate built by the local authority in the 1930s, in part to rehouse the families made homeless when Planks was demolished.

Central Marsden, 1980
Marsden Photographic Archive, courtesy Dave Smith

New Mills and Lakeside

New Mills ceased to weave cloth in 1964/5 and the mill converted to the production of synthetic carpet yarn. This change led to the mill being known as the Mackie Plant because all the new equipment was made by James Mackie of Belfast although the business traded under the names Crowther Bruce & Co. and, later, The Colne Valley Spinning Co. New Mills finally closed in 2001 when Crowthers moved the spinning of carpet yarn up to Bank Bottom Mill. Part of the building is now let off in small units but most of this huge property stands empty until a valid use can be found for it.

New Mills closed in 2001 and still stands almost empty.
Judi Thorpe 2013

The 1848 tithe map shows that Brougham Road follows its present route into the village and, along its southern side, reading from left to right can be seen the Wesleyan Chapel, built in 1824, the Town School built in 1820 and the old cottages dating from 1797 which are still present. Behind them is another group of buildings in what was then called Goodall's Yard.

Enoch Taylor had his first blacksmith's shop in this yard before going on to establish his business at Ready Carr on Carrs Road. The George and Dragon was adjacent to the Taylor's workshop and many invoices, dating from the early 1820s, exist showing the purchase of meat, flour, soap, spirits, tea and coffee. Beer was bought from the Lockwood Brewery, coal from Beeston Manor Iron and Coal Works and nutmeg, cinnamon, ginger and pepper from the Huddersfield shop of George Hall, Chemist and Druggist. On its closure the building was converted into four cottages with a barn, and stables. Idle Row was the old name for most of Brougham Road. The very top part was called Green Bower, a name still attached to the properties on the corner of Brougham Road and Manchester Road.

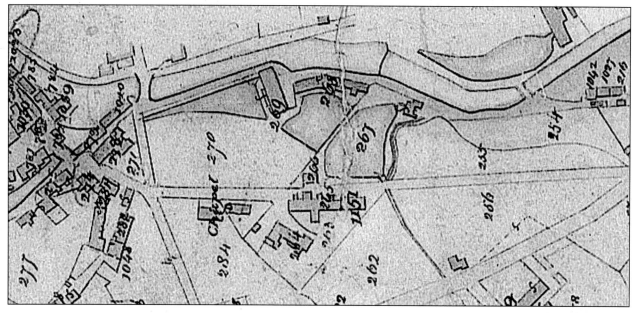

Detail of the 1848 Marsden-in-Almondbury Tithe Map showing the buildings to the south of Brougham Road.

The Factory/Silk Mill and Upper End Mill

John Haigh, a cotton manufacturer, was a highly respected resident of Marsden. He operated his business from four mills, two on the New Mills site and a further two north of the River Colne. They were the Factory, later called the Silk Mill, fronting onto Warehouse Hill and the adjacent Upper End Mill at what is now known as Lakeside. He is best remembered for his employment of pauper children from poor houses in London and Halstead in Essex. Between 1792 and 1803 he brought nearly a hundred children to work for him at the Factory and was reported to the Governors of the Workhouse Board in London for the extreme cruelty to which the children were subjected. Following his bankruptcy the Factory and Upper End Mill were sold at auction along with the Old Corn Mill and Franks Mill. The Leeds Mercury advertised the sale:

MARSDEN MILLS, &c.
To be SOLD by AUCTION

At the George Inn in Huddersfield, on Tuesday the Twelfth Day of December, 1809, due to bankruptcy of Mr. John Haigh.

Lot 1. All that Capital MILL, called Upper End Mill, 127' x 30'. Four storeys high besides Garrets with the Dye-House and Drying Stove also a well-furnished Messuage with a Garden and Reservoir adjoining. The MILL is turned by a Water Wheel 16' in diameter by 12' broad besides which, at the end of the MILL near the Canal is a Patent Steam Engine considered to equal the power of 24 Horses which was originally set up for the Purpose of turning the Machinery of this Mill and in the Factory mentioned in the next Lot, in very dry seasons.

Lot 11. All that Substantial BUILDING called the Factory, 90' x 30'. Four storeys High besides Garrets with an adjoining Winding Shop, 22' x 7' and a newly erected Four-stall Stable with Hay Loft and a Yard adjoining with a Right of Road in Front of the said Factory.

The above two Lots are Leasehold of the Manor of Marsden for a Term of 999 years of which about 22 only are expired at the annual Rent of 16 Guineas.

This sketchy but credible map shows the Factory, Upper End Mill (highlighted) and the mill pond on the north bank of the River Colne. The purpose of the map was to record the owners of properties along the route of the proposed canal, hence the name 'Haigh'.

It is probable that both mills were built in 1787 when Haigh negotiated their leases with the Lord of the Manor of Marsden. The mill buildings are shown to be at right angles to each other but separate.

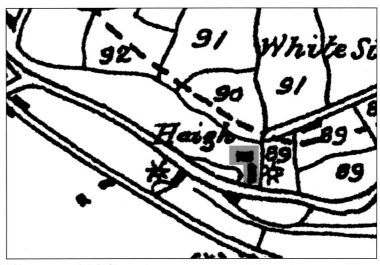

Canal Company survey – 1793
Ref. QDP6 (CALS)

New Mills and Lakeside

The Factory, with its many windows, although not actually located in the Almondbury Parish, was proudly illustrated on the Marsden-in-Almondbury Township map.

Upper End Mill was built into the hillside so that, while the ground floor measured 90' x 30', the two upper storeys measured 129' x 30' and, thus, appear to be joined at right angles to the Factory.

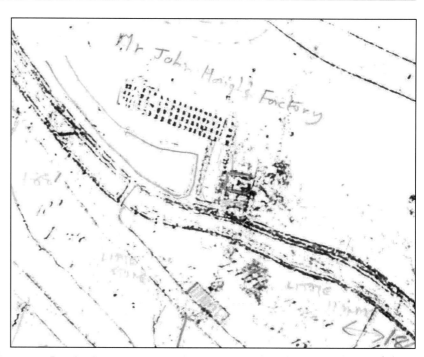

Detail of the Marsden-in-Almondbury Township Map - 1801

The map below shows Upper End Mill at the eastern end of the mill pond with the Factory apparently joined on at right angles to it. This representation of the two mills abutting each other, as shown on both of the township maps remains constant for at least the next 90 years. 'Mr Haigh' s Estate' is written across the site.

Note the footbridge now crossing the River Colne by the mill dam. This 'narrow rickety old structure' was later known as Farrar' s Bridge, after Joshua Farrar who took over Upper End Mill following Haigh's bankruptcy in 1806.

Immediately to the east of Upper End Mill is a field labelled as belonging to Mr. James which is called Kiln Field. It may have been a lime kiln and could account for the name Kiln Lane given to the early footpath into the village which ran alongside the River Colne in this area.

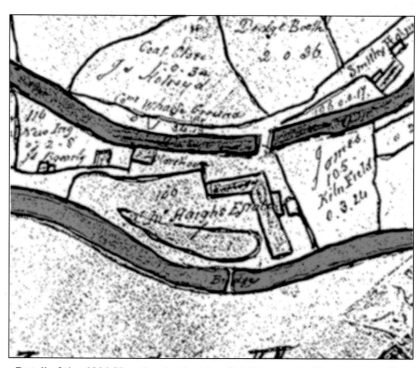

Detail of the 1801 Marsden-in-Huddersfield Township Map showing the canal and The River Colne to the south of it.

New Mills and Lakeside

Detail of O.S. Map - 1854

This is the first map of the site which we can confidently trust. The buildings and mill pond are shown exactly. The configuration of the two mills is shown as an 'L' shape. This map agrees well with the 1850 Tithe Map.

Following the change of ownership of the two mills in 1806, the Factory was converted to the spinning of silk yarn and employed 23 people in the 1841 census rising to over double this number by 1851. This change from cotton to silk led to the building being known as the Silk Mill right up to its demolition some 130 years later. Upper End Mill was shared between two woollen milling enterprises.

The whole site is labelled 'Upper End Mill Silk and Woollen'. The weir, which enabled water to be taken off the River Colne to feed the mill pond, is marked, as is a garden which lies below the Silk Mill and a small terrace of housing which exists to this day to the west of the site.

Kiln Lane, the old footpath which predated Brougham Road as the main thoroughfare into the village from the east, is still evident although Brougham Road had by this time grown in importance. This photograph shows the remnants of the old track looking up from Lakeside towards Manchester Road. Up to at least 250 years ago Kiln Lane was the main thoroughfare leading from Lakeside, over the present day Manchester Road and continuing up the hill on the cobbled foot path which is still used regularly as a cut-through to the village from Gatehead.

The original road into Marsden from the Huddersfield direction was Kiln Lane/ Lodging House Lane.
Judi Thorpe 2013

New Mills and Lakeside

Detail from a view taken in the early 1890s of the Silk Mill and Upper End Mill.
Marsden Photograph Archive

A photograph taken in the early 1890s shows the only view we have of the two mills joined together. In the foreground is Upper End Mill before it was reduced to its present height and length.

To the east of the Silk Mill is a smaller building with a chimney - the engine house referred to in the 1809 auction sale advertisement reproduced earlier. This abuts the three-story eastern end of the Silk Mill (largely obscured by a tree). The garden in front of the mill and the tenter posts are also pictured.

The photograph, below, was taken looking east towards the gable end of the Silk Mill. The square chimney at the far end of the mill belongs to the engine house. The track leading to Lakeside can be seen running in front of the tenter posts, erected sometime in the early 19th century after Upper End Mill converted from cotton to woollen textile production. Some of these posts survive and are graced with their own blue plaque. The building on the left is the wharfinger's cottage and canal warehouse which gave Warehouse Hill its name. This property remains and is now two houses.

Warehouse Hill Tenter Posts – c1890.
Marsden Photographic Archive

New Mills and Lakeside

The 1904 O.S. map identifies the site as 'Warehouse Hill Mills (Woollen)'. Although the name 'Silk Mill' remained in local usage, silk production had ceased by 1880 as woollen textiles became the only product of Marsden mills.

A new bridge has been built across the River Colne, slightly upstream of the now demolished Farrar's Bridge, with a road connecting it to Warehouse Hill. Extensive changes have taken place to the mill buildings which are now shown as two separate properties.

The terrace of houses at the western end have been extended to join up with the Silk Mill and, just below, are two more blocks of terrace housing.

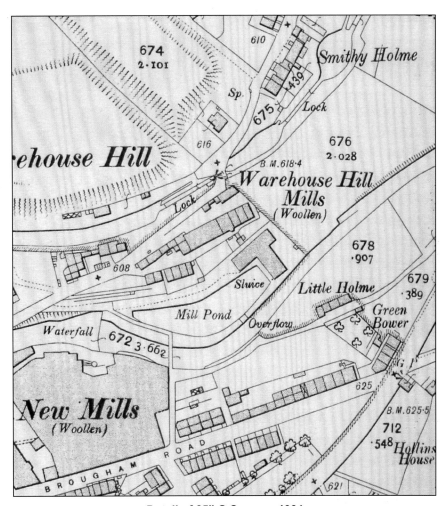

Detail of 25" O.S. map - 1904

The rear of Colne Terrace.
Roger Logue 2011

The map also shows that Colne Terrace has now been built onto the eastern end of the mill. The stone columns which support the balcony in front of this terrace were once part of the old church in Towngate. All these houses remained after the Silk Mill was demolished in 1938 and are still in occupation today.

New Mills and Lakeside

The mill pond which fed the Upper End Mill water wheel explains the name of Lakeside.
Marsden Photographic Archive – c1920

The photograph above is taken from the southern side of the River Colne, looking towards Warehouse Hill. It probably dates from the early 1920s when the telephone arrived in Marsden - telegraph poles are visible as evidence. The mill pond, which gave rise to this area being called Lakeside, is in the left foreground. The Silk Mill is in the centre with Colne Terrace on the extreme right. Upper End Mill has now been reduced to two storeys although it is not known when this occurred.

This view shows that the mill pond has been filled in and is now a car park. Despite the total absence of water, this area is still known as Lakeside.

The Silk Mill only remains as an empty space between houses. Upper End Mill, although much reduced from its original size, has been used by various organisations over the years. For example, it was a hostel for Polish ex-servicemen who came to Marsden to work in the mills after World War II, and, during the 1970/80s, it housed the Youth Club.

The building is currently in daily use as a day nursery and pre-school playgroup.

Bird's eye view of the Lakeside area
© Google Earth

New Mills and Lakeside

This photograph shows the site of the Silk Mill at the present time. The brick gable end of Colne Terrace was built when the mill was demolished in 1938.

The cobbled path which led from the mill up to Warehouse Hill remains as the sole relic. The gabled roof on the building at the bottom of the steps is the remaining part of Upper End Mill.

Site of the Silk Mill.
Judi Thorpe 2012

This view is taken from the rear of the building. Upper End Mill is still the same two-storey building shown in the earlier black and white photograph.

However, when viewed from Lakeside car park, only one storey is exposed, the ground level having been built up. The green painted taking-in door which is seen in the earlier photograph, is just visible through the vegetation.

Upper End Mill.
Judi Thorpe 2012

Chapter 4 - The Mills along the Wessenden Brook

There were three old mills on the Wessenden Brook which predated the arrival of what we now know as Bank Bottom Mill. They were Upper Bank Bottom, Lower Bank Bottom and Ottiwells.

Detail from the 1854 O.S. Map showing the three mills in the lower Wessenden Valley.

The Mills along the Wessenden Brook

Upper Bank Bottom Mill – 'Top Bonk'

The mill, still referred to as 'Top Bonk', was built by the time the 1801 Township map of Marsden-in-Almondbury was produced. It was a scribbling and carding mill which prepared the wool ready for spinning. The spinning and weaving of cloth were originally activities undertaken by handloom weavers and their families in their own homes. An auction catalogue from c1820 described Upper Bank Bottom Mill as being,

> **'Three Stories high, besides the Attic, 74 Feet 6 Inches in length, and 34 Feet 6 Inches in breadth, with a Fall of 22 Feet 6 Inches on the Wessenden River, the Willow House at the West-end of the said Mill, with the Boiler and Steam Pipes, Water Wheel, Going Gear, Dam, Weirs and Water-courses'**

The mill changed hands again in 1851 when Norris, Sykes and Fisher sold it along with Lower Bank Bottom Mill due to the *'intended retirement from business of one of the proprietors'*.

The advertisement in the Leeds Mercury dated 4th October 1851 said,

> **'The mill called Upper Mill is worked by a very powerful wheel of modern construction, 28 feet 6 inches in diameter by 12 feet wide, with a never-failing supply of water, and about 35 horses power.'**

In 1869 both Upper and Lower Bank Bottom Mills, then owned by Benjamin Sykes and Sons, were again sold. The upper mill had been enlarged and was described in the 18th August 1869 edition of the Leeds Mercury auction details as,

> **'All that FREEHOLD WOOLLEN MILL, called Upper Bank Bottom, three and four storeys high together with the willey room, wheel house, and capital iron wheel having a fall of 27 feet, and a never-failing supply of water for motive power, augmented by storage in a large reservoir, and all that substantial BUILDING called the Weaving and Spinning Mill, three storeys high.'**

Upper Bank Bottom Mill. Courtesy of Colne Valley Museum from the Clifford Westerby collection

The Mills along the Wessenden Brook

It should be noted that the mill had, by 1869, become a place where cloth was produced rather than merely finished, handloom weaving based in the weaver's home having been largely replaced as industrialisation took over. It was said that '*skilled labour necessary for all purposes can be had from the village of Marsden and the surrounding districts*'. The advertisement went on to say that both Upper and Lower Bank Bottom mills were

> **'.... admirably adapted for carrying on a large business in the manufacture of woollen fabrics. The mills, being the highest on the Wessenden brook, are first takers of one of the best supplies of pure soft water in the kingdom, and the supply is constant during every working day of the year. The water is derived from the Wessenden Reservoir (constructed under the powers of a special Act of Parliament), which contains about 110 millions of gallons, and is fed by a large drainage area. This supply is increased by numerous springs and tributary streams.'**

Wessenden 'Old' Reservoir was completed in 1790 by local mill owners, specifically to ensure a constant supply of water to their mills lower down the valley. This group of mill owners were known as the Wessenden Commissioners, and they enlarged the reservoir between 1837 and 1842. They sold it to Huddersfield Corporation in 1890 for £50,000.

Whitehead, in his book 'Bygone Marsden', says that, prior to its demolition, Upper Bank Bottom Mill was '*a curious old building, having many irregular parts that suggested various additions and partial demolitions. There was no harmony of line about the structure, which seemed to have grown by fits and starts and over all there was a general impression of unkemptness.*'

The increase in the population throughout the Huddersfield area demanded a more abundant supply of drinking water. Huddersfield Corporation purchased Upper and Lower Bank Bottom mills in 1890 for the sum of £50,000 in preparation for the construction of Butterley Reservoir.

Upper Bank Bottom Mill during demolition.
Courtesy of Colne Valley Museum from the Clifford Westerby collection

The Mills along the Wessenden Brook

Upper Bank Bottom mill was demolished and replaced by the embankment and spillway that exists today.

This photograph was taken looking down the spillway of Butterley Reservoir towards the site of Lower Bank Bottom Mill. Bank Bottom Bridge is in the centre of the image.

The house on the right-hand side, Glenholme, was built by Huddersfield Corporation as accommodation for the resident Waterman. It seems likely that extensive alterations will shortly be made to the spillway despite objections being made by many people.

Butterley Reservoir spillway
Judi Thorpe 2013

Lower Bank Bottom Mill

Lower Bank Bottom Mill was built by Abraham and John Horsfall sometime before 1801. The Horsfall brothers also owned Ottiwells Mill and House further downstream. The auction catalogue c1820 describes Lower Bank Bottom Mill as being,

> **'A Fulling and Scribbling Mill, three Stories high, besides the Attic, 46 Feet 6 Inches in length, and 31 Feet 6 in breadth, with a Fall of 17 Feet 11 Inches on the Wessenden River; together with Fulling Stocks, Water Wheel, Going Gear, Dam, Weirs, and Water-courses; and also the Blacksmith And Carpenter's Shop.'**

Lower Bank Bottom Mill is shown on the 1854 O.S. map. Bank Bottom Bridge provided access for traffic to and from the mill via a track leading down to Binn Road. This track is now a designated public footpath.

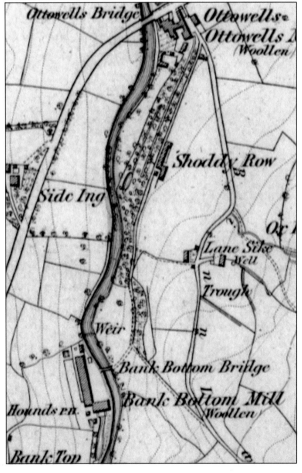

Lower Bank Bottom Mill and Bank Bottom Bridge on the Wessenden Brook
Detail from the 1854 O.S. map

The Mills along the Wessenden Brook

The photograph below shows Lower Bank Bottom Mill prior to its demolition. The houses in the background were built on Mount Road by the Huddersfield Corporation Water Board in conjunction with the building of Butterley Reservoir.

Lower Bank Bottom Mill. Courtesy of Colne Valley Museum from the Clifford Westerby collection.

An auction of the mill was held on 29th October 1851. The Leeds Mercury carried a full description of the property,

> **'The Mill is worked by a powerful wheel, 20 feet in diameter by 6 feet wide, with a never-failing supply of water, and about 14 horses power. The premises embrace scribbling and slubbing, weaving and spinning rooms, dye houses, wool and tenter stoves with the needful boiler houses and boilers, warehouses and counting houses, gas works, sheds and various outbuildings.'**

During the thirty years or so prior to this last description many developments had taken place driven by the advance of the industrialisation of the woollen industry. The mill had become a place of cloth production rather than being merely a fulling mill and a gas works had been constructed on the property probably to provide lighting. The advertisement also emphasised that the mill was 'well roaded' and near to the railway and the canal. The property was said to be in a 'most complete state of repair in all its parts and was filled up with machinery of the most modern and ample'. Unfortunately this was not to last. On 20th March 1858 the Leeds Mercury reported that the mill had had a fire. Whitehead, in 'Bygone Marsden', relates that 'one length of the mill was burnt down creating something of a record among mill fires. The mill was rebuilt with considerable extensions'.

The Mills along the Wessenden Brook

Lower Bank Bottom Mill c. 1892
Marsden Photographic Archive

Joseph, William and Elon Crowther, trading as John Crowther and Sons, rented Lower Bank Bottom Mill in 1867 and started producing woollen cloth. From this early, modest beginning grew what was, at one time, the largest, privately-owned, woollen cloth producing business in the country. In 1891 Huddersfield Corporation purchased the mill as part of the Butterley Reservoir project referred to above and used the main building as a storehouse. On completion of the reservoir the mill remained empty and was finally demolished in 1913. A house and storage buildings now occupy the site which is at the bottom of the Butterley Reservoir spillway at the end of the track leading from Binn Road. The houses at the beginning of this trackway are known as Shady Row. This name is a relic of an earlier row of cottages, shown on the 1854 O.S. map as Shoddy Row, which were built closer to Lower Bank Bottom Mill. This original terrace was demolished to make room for the expansion of what is now known as Bank Bottom Mill.

Ottiwells Mill

The name Ottiwells survives to this day in the memory of the house and mill which once occupied the site at the bottom of Binn Road. The bridge over the Wessenden Brook at the bottom of Mount Road is still called Ottiwells Bridge and the lowest of the three rows of terraced houses at the bottom of Binn Road built in the early 1900s to house textile workers is called Ottiwells Terrace.

It is probable that Ottiwells was the place occupied by one Othuel Marsden who died in 1589. Parish registers show that Ottiwelle or Ottuel continued to be the home of a family with the surname Marsden for years after Othuel Marsden died.

Ottiwells Mill was built in 1793 after the Manor of Marsden granted a 1000 year copyhold lease for the land. Its architecture is similar to other early mills in the area which were built before the later building style for mills was established.

The Mills along the Wessenden Brook

Abraham and John Horsfall owned a considerable acreage of farmland in the area and built the mill so as to extend their activities into the fulling of woollen cloth which had been woven in cottages around the village.

An auction catalogue c1820 describes the mill as being,

'A Fulling Mill, adjoining the Turnpike Road, two Stories high, 129 Feet in length, and 27 Feet 6 Inches in breadth, with a Fall of 20 Feet 3 Inches on the Wessenden river; together with the Boiler and Steam Pipes, Fulling Stocks, Two Water Wheels, Going Gear, Dam, Weirs, and Goits.'

A weir, upstream of the mill and a goit (highlighted in blue on the map on the right), which runs down to the mill, are evident on the 1801 Township map.

In 1810 the tragedy of the Black Flood, of which more later, resulted in *'the death of the miller's wife'* and the inundation of the mill.

Two years after the flood an even more dramatic misfortune occurred. Cropping frames, made at the nearby Taylor's blacksmith's shop, were installed in the mill in early 1812 and this substitution of machinery for hand labour attracted the deep animosity of the Luddites. Fearing that the mill would be attacked the Horsfalls erected a barricade in front of the mill.

The Huddersfield Examiner of 26th December 1863 wrote,
'At Ottiwells, at the upper end of the road fronting the mill, and on an elevation, level with the present dam, a cannon was planted behind a wall pierced with openings three feet high and ten inches wide. Through these apertures, the cannon could be pointed so as to command the entire footage of the mill and fired upon an approaching enemy. This somewhat primitive battery still exists, but the artillery disappeared long ago; and though now walled up, the outlines of the embrasures formerly left for the cannon to be discharged through may yet be discerned.'

The 1801 Township map shows Ottiwells Mill (highlighted in pink).

Ottiwells Mill shortly before demolition. The 'primitive battery' is the structure on the left
Marsden Photographic Archive

The mill was never attacked, however the '*enemy*' found another target. William Horsfall, a family member of the business, was determined that he would not be intimidated and boasted that '*he would like to ride up to his saddle girths in Luddite blood*'. In April 1812 he was shot on Crosland Moor while riding home and died soon afterwards of his injuries. The cropping frames were removed from the mill.

The 1854 O.S. map clearly shows the mill. Shoddy Row, built to house millworkers, had also been erected on the track running from Ottiwells Mill to Lower Bank Bottom Mill. Later maps refer to this terrace of houses as Shady Row and it is thought 'Shoddy' was the dialect pronunciation of Shady.

Ottiwells mill became redundant and stood unused from about 1860 until it was demolished in 1876. Fisher sold the building in 1865, probably to Messrs. John Crowther and Sons, although this has not been verified. The site was eventually developed by the Crowthers to further extend Marsden Mills as they were called before the Crowther mill complex became known as Bank Bottom Mill.

The Mills along the Wessenden Brook

Ottiwells House

The new turnpike route, constructed during the 1780s and 1790s, bypassed the village centre, ran along Carrs Road, over Ottiwells bridge and up Mount Road. Ottiwells Bridge was built by John Metcalf, the famous blind surveyor, more usually known as Blind Jack of Knaresborough. Such was the increase in traffic that coaching inns were built to accommodate travellers. Ottiwells House, built at the junction of Mount Road and Binn Road, was originally a coaching inn called The George and was run by Thomas Chippendale. However, by the early 1800s it was the residence of the two Horsfall families who built the adjoining mills.

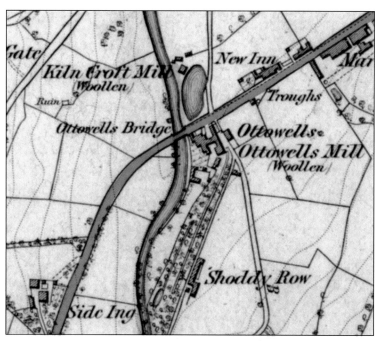
Detail from the 1854 O.S. map showing the Turnpike route in red

An early auction catalogue described the building as being,

'A Substantial Messuage or Dwelling House near the Turnpike Road leading from Huddersfield to Manchester, with the Barn, Stable, Cowhouse, and other Outbuildings, Garden and Yards therewith Occupied'.

Ottiwells House was originally built as a coaching inn along the Turnpike route.
Marsden Photographic Archive

The house changed hands over the years and seems to have had more than one household in occupation at any one time. The 1841 census shows the it to have been occupied by both William Kinder, a woollen manufacturer and his family, and by John Talents Fisher, a cloth merchant, and his footman and other servants. Ottiwells House was demolished in 1912 by the current owners, the Crowthers, to make way for a bowling green for the enjoyment of their workforce.

The Mills along the Wessenden Brook

The Black Flood

In 1810 The Gentlemen's Magazine reported that, *'the reservoir at the top of Standedge in Marsden, about nine miles west of Huddersfield, burst, and the water flowing in an easterly direction, innundated the whole of the adjoining valley.'* The reservoir in question was later said to be Swellands Reservoir (also called Swillers and Swine Clough) although recent work by Geoff Brown of Saddleworth Historical Society has shown that it was the Black Moss Reservoir that burst; Swellands was not built until after the date of the flood.

Ottiwells House was among the properties at Bank Bottom which were affected by *'the destructive impetuosity'* of the water. The article in the Gentleman's Magazine went on to say,

'Rushing forward in its fatal course, the water advanced to the mill of Messrs. Horsfall, and so completely inundated the house of the miller that himself and his wife were floated out of their bed; he seized the stonework in the window, and for some time he held his wife in his embrace, but she was at length swum from him, and her lifeless body was taken up the next morning at a place called Paddock, two miles from Huddersfield; the husband, however, kept his hold of the window till the water subsided, and by that means preserved his life.'

Although this is a colourful account, Geoff Brown's researches showed that the victim was probably the wife of a mill employee called Balmforth. It should also be said that the flood claimed the lives of five members of the Haigh family from a house higher up the Wessenden Valley.

The course of the 'Black Flood' of 1810. Black Moss Reservoir is at
bottom left, Ottiwells House stood at top right.
Note: Butterley and Swellands Reservoirs
had not been built at the time of the flood.
Image © Google Earth

The Mills along the Wessenden Brook

The Bank Bottom Mills of the Crowther Years

The Crowther dynasty is well known in the village. Over the years they were major employers and benefactors in Marsden. Their connection with textile production in Marsden began in 1867 when they rented Lower Bank Bottom Mill.

Whitehead heralds this beginning by saying that Messrs. John Crowther and Sons, '*made the place hum with a new commercial life, that not only established a reputation of the Crowther brothers for great business capacity but proved a stepping stone to personal fortune*'.

Having built a new mill between Lower Bank Bottom Mill and Ottiwells Mill they moved into their new premises and continued to expand rapidly. The 1895 map shows the extent of Bank Bottom Mills owned and occupied by Messrs. John Edward Crowther Ltd. at that time. The business continued to grow and expand, reaching a peak in the early 1900s. The six storey building was completed in 1910 and was exclusively used for spinning.

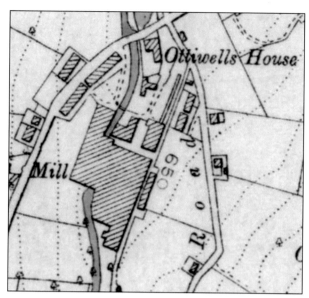

The 1895 O.S. map shows the extent of Bank Bottom Mills owned and occupied by Messrs. John Edward Crowther & Sons at that time.

Crowther's Bank Bottom Mill expanded to reach its peak in the early 1900s.
Marsden Photographic Archive

The Mills along the Wessenden Brook

This image of mill workers leaving Bank Bottom Mills indicates the number of employees
who worked at Bank Bottom in the late 1800s.
Marsden Photographic Archive

The Crowthers were the largest employers in Marsden. A fire which gutted the twisting sheds in 1909 was reported to have resulted in 1,000 people being temporarily thrown out of work.

The firm built houses for their employees. Spring Street and Royds Street are shown on the 1908 O.S. map. Ottiwells Terrace was also in existence at the time, having been built in 1907, but the row of houses was not present when the map was surveyed.

The business also incorporated an old mill on Fall Lane which was present as early as 1818 according to Greenwood`s map of that date. The 1854 O.S. map shows Kiln Croft Mill and dam between the Wessenden River and Fall Lane.

This mill was known as Old Isaac's Mill after a one-time owner, Isaac Bottomley. In 1871 it was briefly taken over by William and Elon Crowther, sons of John Edward, before they moved to Slaithwaite to establish the firm of W. and E. Crowther.

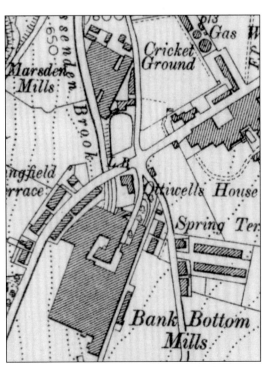

1908 O.S. map. The rapid growth in terrace housing near to the mills is evidence that textile workers often rented their houses from their employers.

107

The Mills along the Wessenden Brook

John Edward Crowther and Sons took over the old mill building which they demolished in 1903. They used the site to build a new mill and engine house which became known as Marsden Mill or Fall Lane Mill.

The building became largely obsolete and remained empty for many years. It was completely destroyed by fire in 1984. A sports hall and large warehouse now occupy the site. There is still a dam on the site although it was partially covered by a Dining Room for Crowther employees.

Fall Lane Mill burned down in 1984.
Judi Thorpe 1984

The Dining Room was built in 1905 supported above the water on iron posts. When opened it was claimed to be '*second to none*' in the country.

The 'dining room' for Crowther employees, fronting on to Mount Road.
Marsden Photographic Archive

The Mills along the Wessenden Brook

The general decline in the woollen textile industry affected all the mills in Marsden. In 1975 Bank Bottom Mill ceased to make cloth but continued in a small way spinning and dyeing carpet yarn until all production ceased in 2003. The buildings remain as a reminder of the time when Bank Bottom Mill was part of the Crowther's textile business which was recognised as one of the largest privately owned textile concerns in the country. In their prime Crowther's cloth was admired and exported world wide.

In addition to the premises at Bank Bottom, Crowthers also owned Ready Carr Mill which they purchased when Taylor's Iron Foundry closed, Fall Lane Mill, otherwise known as Marsden Mill, and later, New Mills on Brougham Road.

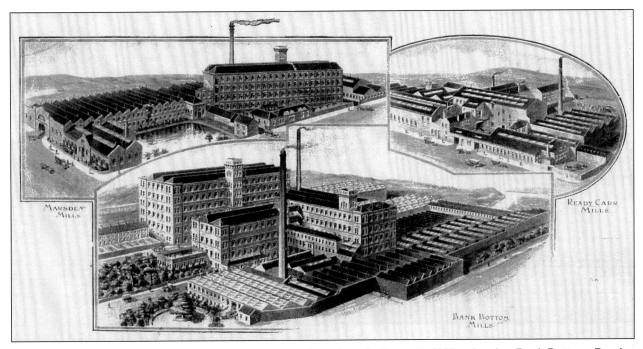

Engraving from publicity produced by John Edward Crowthers in the early 1900s showing Bank Bottom, Ready Carr and Marsden Mills, more commonly known as Fall Lane Mill.

Chapter 5 - Development along Carrs Road

The completion of Carrs Road, as part of the second Turnpike route, stimulated new developments in this part of the village. This included The New Inn and Ready Carr House, both of which are shown on the 1801 Township map. They were built as coaching inns, along with Ottiwells House, to cater for the increase in traffic along the new road. The Leeds Mercury dated 13th February, 1841 offered the lease of The New Inn which was described as being '*old established*' but of '*recent erection*'. The original building, dating from around 1780, had been demolished and the site used for the erection of the buillding present today. At that time it was an extensive property having

> '**a spacious Yard, Stabling for Twenty-four Horses, Cow-houses, Lock up Carriage House, and other Outbuildings and Appurtenances. The House contains Four Sitting Rooms, Seven Bed Rooms, a commodious Bar; large Kitchen, with Scullery and Wash-house; excellent Wine, Porter, Ale and Beer Cellars; Larder and other Conveniences; with an abundant Supply of excellent Water. Ten coaches daily stop for change of Horses, besides which the superior nature of the Accommodation for Gentlemen's Travelling Carriages and Horses secures a most respectable Business, not only during the Summer Season, but throughout the Year.**'

At the time of this advertisement the new Turnpike along Manchester Road had opened and the business must have faced severe competition from the relocation of traffic onto the new route. The property became known as the Old New Inn following the erection of the new New Inn on Manchester Road.

The Old New Inn remained as a licensed public house until 2011 when it was converted into two houses. It is sited on the northern side of Carrs Road near to Ottiwells.

The former Old New Inn built in c1840 on the site of an earlier coaching inn.
Judi Thorpe 2012

Development along Carrs Road

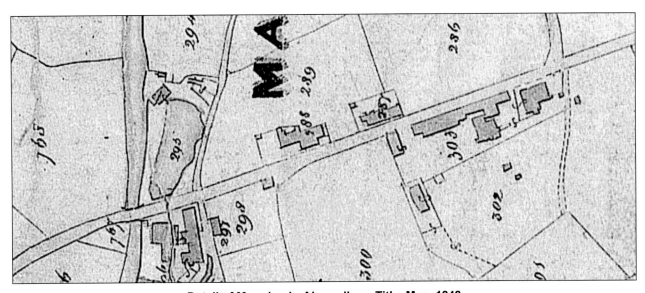

Detail of Marsden-in-Almondbury Tithe Map, 1848.
Carrs Road runs diagonally across the map with the Old New Inn and Chorley Row on the northern side and Ready Carr House and early development of the Foundry to the south

Chorley Row, which first appears on the 1848 Tithe map, is adjacent to the Old New Inn and is still in occupation,

Ready Carr House was originally called The Red Lion. It was one of the several inns in or near the village used to quarter the soldiery who were stationed in Marsden to protect people and property during the Luddite riots in 1812.

The remuneration allowed by the Government for the maintenance of the soldiers was reported to be so inadequate that the innkeepers were impoverished and, in some cases, ruined. It was also claimed that the presence of these troops led to The Red Lion's loss of favour as a hostelry.

Chorley Row is still in occupation some 150 years after being built.
Judi Thorpe 2012

Whatever the reason the Red Lion closed as an inn and, in 1813, the building became the home and place of work of the Taylor family and its name was changed to Ready Carr House.

Enoch Taylor and his brother, James, relocated their metal working business from Goodall's Yard in Brougham Road and established the beginnings of Marsden Iron Foundry. They used the back part of the house as a blacksmith's shop and located a millwright's shop on the third floor of the house. The stabling and barn, previously attached to the coaching inn, were converted into a foundry. As the business prospered so the foundry buildings became more extensive until they spread along Carrs Road towards Ottiwells.

Development along Carrs Road

Ready Carr House is far left of centre, with North View Cottages and the Foundry to its right.
Detail of old postcard c1900
Marsden Photographic Archive

The two brothers and their successors produced a wide range of products which included waterwheels, bridges, railings, steam boilers, engines, looms and mill gearing. They also held a licence to make the cropping frames which were installed in Ottiwells Mill and provoked the Luddite activity in this area. The products of the Iron Foundry were sold throughout Yorkshire and Lancashire and beyond. The Marsden foundry made the iron bridges and railings which border the Wessenden and Colne rivers.

The Towngate Bridge and the railings on Weirside, made by Taylor's foundry.
Judi Thorpe 2012

Development along Carrs Road

In common with other major employers in Marsden, Taylor's built houses for their workers.

A terrace of nine cottages, known as North View, was built in 1898 on the site of a surplus machine shop. These are shown on the 1894 O.S. map.

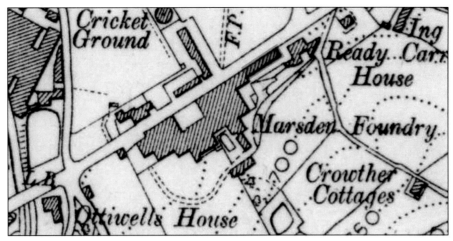

Detail from the 1894 O.S. map showing North View

When the business ceased Ready Carr House, North View cottages and the Iron Foundry premises were sold at auction in 1905 to Messrs John Edward Crowther.

In 1914 Crowther's sold Ready Carr House to the Adult School Trust. Part of the building was turned into a hostel for Polish ex-servicemen who came to Marsden in 1945/6 to work in the mills. In 1971 the building became so dangerous that it was condemned by the council and was demolished.

Crowther's used the industrial buildings as a rag mill, renamed Ready Carr Mill, until the mid 1980s when the site was cleared and they developed the area for private housing. North View cottages were also demolished and the site, together with adjacent land to the south of Carrs Road became an extensive new housing estate. A terrace of shops, with living accommodation above, near to Fall Lane roundabout was built by Crowther's in 1910 and remains to this day.

Ready Carr House, North View cottages and the Marsden Foundry have all been demolished and replaced by private housing along and to the south of Carrs Road.

Judi Thorpe 2013

Development along Carrs Road

To the east of the site of Ready Carr House is a row of old cottages. The pathway between them and the grounds of the imposing Crow Hill leads to a house which was once a smithy. When Marsden Park was being created in 1912, Dan Ineson, the blacksmith who owned this smithy, also owned a shed on the piece of land now occupied by the War Memorial.

He refused to sell this land unless he could erect another shed in the grounds of Inner Hey. Understandably, the owner, Mr John Bower Robinson, was reluctant to allow his garden to be invaded. On the death of 'Old Dan' the land was acquired and incorporated into the park.

Dan Ineson's smithy off Carrs Road
Judi Thorpe 2013

Beyond the grounds of Crow Hill there was ribbon development of housing at the eastern end of Carrs Road dating from the early 1900s. Carrs Street, behind Carrs Road, was created in 1936 after the site had been cleared by the demolition of an old mill. 'Bleachers Mill', as it was commonly called, served many purposes, including dyeing, bleaching and rug-making.

Bleacher's Mill and its dam are in the left foreground
Marsden Photographic Archive

The village today

The textile industry began to decline seriously in the 1960s. In order to help mills to become more competitive, government grants were made available to replace outdated Dobcross looms with the hugely more efficient Rapier looms, on condition that the old looms were scrapped rather than being sold on. Unfortunately this boost to production was short-lived as cheaper woollen cloth flooded in from Europe. There was a continuing decline and mills started to close or contract. Crowthers, were the last textile firm in the village to close in 2001/2. This was a sad day for Marsden which had relied on the production of cloth for generations as a source of employment. The frequency of the bus service to Huddersfield and the increase of car ownership allowed people living in Marsden to find work outside the village. It was also fortunate that the Beeching cuts had spared Marsden station which lies on a main trans-Pennine route. This made the village an attractive place to live for commuters working in Manchester or Leeds.

The face of Marsden has changed dramatically in the last 40 years from an industrial village to become a dormitory community with little employment other than in retail and services. During this period many new houses have been built by private builders, some, such as the Clough Lea estate, on the site of demolished mills, others extending on roads leading away from the village and the Deer Hill development which was partially on a green field site. The 'in-comers', despite initially being treated with suspicion, became integrated and, it should be said, brought with them enthusiasm and energy which has added to the life of the village by their participation in existing groups. Marsden is exceptional in that the village had a large number of long-established clubs, churches and societies already in existence before it began to change in the 1970s. These included the Parish Church Amateur Operatic and Dramatic Society, the cricket, golf and football clubs and the brass band.

Apart from being a place for commuters Marsden's other role is, possibly, a more important one. The range of activities available to locals and visitors alike brings tourists into the village.

Such attractions as the annual Marsden Jazz Festival, Imbolc, Marsden Cuckoo Day, the Walkers are Welcome initiative, National Trust guided walks and plant sales and regular dramatic and musical performances all bring large numbers of people in.

All visitors sustain the economy by spending money in the local shops, pubs and cafes which helps to ensure that these businesses remain viable and available to locals after the visitors have left.

Jack Frost, the symbol of Winter, at the Imbolc Festival
Keith Hemsley 2009

Improvements to the richness of life in the village were often brought about by a combination of old and new residents working together. The reopening of the canal was largely the initiative of members of the Canal Society. Due to their efforts visitors can, once again travel along the canal by boat to Tunnel End and its Visitors' Centre and even experience a guided boat ride into the tunnel.

The Canal Society water taxi ferries visitors to Tunnel End Visitors' Centre
Judi Thorpe 2013

The Mechanics' Institute was saved from threatened demolition by a group of residents and, after a complete renovation was reopened to provide an important venue for meetings, exhibitions, entertainments, weddings, a library and Information Centre. It is likely to become, once again, the sole responsibility of the village under the asset-transfer scheme proposed by Kirklees Council. The regeneration of the park was achieved by the Friends of Marsden Park in time to celebrate the Park's Centenary celebration. The tradition of crown green bowling and brass band concerts in the Bandstand continues but with the added attraction of a playground for children.

Many of these additions and improvements were instigated or supported by the local authority and other bodies but would not have succeeded without the enthusiastic support and involvement of the whole village. The opening of the M62 in 1971 spared Marsden from the incessant heavy freight traffic which used the A62 Manchester Road through the village although the Motormans' Café still continues to provide for travellers.

Marsden is a good place to live and bring up children. It continues to thrive albeit very different in nature to the village that relied on the mills for its prosperity.

Marsden Time Line

c7000 BC	Early Mesolithic hunters present on moors above Marsden
2100 - 750BC	Bronze Age
c79	AD Roman Road built through Marsden
1068	Marchesden awarded to Ilbert de Laci by William I
c1450	St. Bartholomew's first church built in Towngate, was `dilapidated` by 1480
1499	Marsden becomes a manor in its own right
1560	Corn Mill present in middle of village
c1600	White Hart (originally called The Hare and Hounds) in Towngate, delicensed in 1910
1616	Manor House at Highgate
1616	The Hill at West Slaithwaite near Nathans
1641	House off Old Mount Road inscribed IMMI 1641
1666	Hearth Tax Returns show 82 houses with hearths
1679	Date stone at rear of 23 Towngate
1670	Higher Green Owlers at the top of Blakelea Lane in The Dean
1670	White Hull Farm below Higher Green Owlers
1671	Green Top at Pule Side
1673	Clark Hill off Old Mount Rd.
1683	Date stone on now demolished house in Chapel Fold, off Church Lane
1685	Berry Greave Farm
1710	Hey Green Fulling Mill - first textile mill
1711	Binn Lodge near the top of Binn Road
c1721	Towngate Bridge
1722	Far Owlers, on Redbrook Clough below Manchester Road
c1725	The Old Ram Inn at the top of Towngate demolished 1926
1739	Smithy Holme on Marsden Lane
1738	Towngate began to be developed. Date stones on now demolished houses, 1751/52/56/62
1738	17 Towngate
1738	Upper Green Owlers
1739	Hill Top at Binn
1743	Lower Green Owlers on Blakelea Lane
c1745	Planks. Demolition began 1937
1746	Troaves Farm
1751	Binn Lodge Farm
1753	Carr Farm
1754	The Hill, between Meltham Road and Manchester Road
c1756	The Hall (Chapel House), Towngate
1758	Nathans at West Slaithwaite
c1760	First Turnpike route opened
1761	St. Bartholomew's rebuilt – outline of building still visible on the green space in Towngate
1762	Two Dutchmen in Towngate - demolished 1962
1763	The Green cottages
1772	Stubbin Farm on road linking Manchester Road with Carrs Road
1773	Steep Farm near bottom of Meltham Road
1773	White Lea off Manchester Road

1776	Binn Lodge
c1780	Turnpike opened along Carrs Road - 2nd route
c1780	Ottiwells Bridge
1780	Old New Inn, rebuilt in 1840
1780	Old Housend now called Owlers End Farm, Binn Road
c1780	Tommy Mellor's Bridge linking The Green with Clough Lea
1780	Clough Lea cottages
1785	Frank Mill off Brougham Road – original mill of this name demolished 1901
1787	Red Lion in Market Place
1790	Wessenden Old Reservoir
c1790	Upper Bank Bottom Mill
1793	Ottiwells Mill
1793	Ottiwells House, built as a coaching inn called The George
c1795	Corn Mill established at Hey Green
1797	Idle Row cottages - later named Brougham Road
1798	Clough Lea cotton mill rebuilt 1841
1798	Graveyard in Towngate raised to accommodate unprecedented number of burials
1798/99	Snailhorn Bridge replaced 1891
1798	The Factory/Silk Mill on Warehouse Hill, demolished 1938
1798	Upper End Mill at Lakeside
c1800	New Mill off Brougham Road – original mill of this name
c1800	Enoch & James Taylor establish blacksmith business in Goodalls Yard off Brougham Road
1807	Congregational Church, Buckley Hill, rebuilt on present site and again rebuilt in 1931
1807	Sparth Reservoir completed
1807	Black Moss Reservoir under construction
c1810	George and Dragon in Goodalls Yard off Brougham Road
1811	Standedge Canal tunnel opened
1812	Luddite riots, William Horsfall murdered
1820	Town School on Brougham Road, rebuilt 1877 and enlarged in 1902
1824	Wesleyan Methodist Chapel built on Brougham Road rebuilt 1871, demolished 1968
1828	Redbrook Reservoir extended
1829	Church School built on site of present lych gate demolished 1928
1830	Vicarage built, enlarged in 1854
1832	March Haigh Reservoir completed
1835	William Johnstone's first shop at Bridge End, later moved to Peel Street
1838	New Inn on Manchester Road
1839	Turnpike, third route completed (A62)
1839	Hey Green Bridge
c1840s	Sherbrooke Cottages, Manchester Road
1841	Middle Mill on Clough Lea rebuilt on site of earlier mill, demolished in 1996
1842	Wessenden Reservoir enlarged to 19 acres
1849	First railway tunnel opened
1849	Railway Station opened
1852	New burial ground consecrated
1856	National School built at bottom of Old Mount Road, demolished 1967
1856	Gas Works built next to old Ambulance Station on Manchester Road, demolished in 1970s
1861	Union Bridge
1861	Mechanics' Institute

1863	Idle Row renamed Brougham Road
1866	Foundation for new Parish Church – work suspended for 28 yrs
c1870	William Johnstone`s emporium on Peel Street, now the Riverhead Tap and the Wine Bank
1871	New Wesleyan Church built on site of old one in Brougham Road
1871	Second Railway tunnel opened
1874	Thimble Street renamed Argyle Street
1874	Liberal Club on Peel Street, enlarged in 1905
1875	Fall Lane widened and Taylor's Bridge built linking Fall Lane with Towngate
1876	Towngate Bridge rebuilt as now
1879	Derby Terrace, Brougham Road
1881	Wessenden Head Reservoir (1877-1881)
1888	Marsden-in-Almondbury and Marsden-in-Huddersfield united into one parish
1890	Congregational Sunday School, Buckley Hill converted into flats in 2007
1891	Snailhorn Bridge replaced with realignment as now
1898	Peel Street developed on east side
1894	Third (double track) Railway tunnel opened
1894	Waterworks tram road built to carry puddle clay to Blakeley and Butterley reservoir dams
1895	St. Bartholomew's Church consecrated on new site, Bell Tower 1910, Baptistry 1911
1896	Co-op, Market Place
1897	Old burial ground in Towngate closed
c1900	Market Walk terrace housing
1902	Grange Cottages
1904	Blakeley Reservoir completed
1904	New shops in Market Place on site of older shops
1904	Leatholm Royd on Manchester Road
1905	Bank Bottom Dining Room
1906	Butterley Reservoir (1901 -1906)
1906	New Mills on Brougham Road extended over the river
1908	Conservative Club, Victoria Street
1908	Ottiwells House demolished
1909	Fire Station, Manchester Road
1910	Sunny Lea, Manchester Road
1910	Council School, Manchester Road
1911	Socialist Club, Manchester Road
1911	Lower Plains housing
1911	Co-op Stables on Warehouse Hill, now Cavendish Court
1912	Marsden Park
1913	Lower Bank Bottom Mill demolished
1918	Electric Theatre, closed 1975
1914	Ambulance Station, adjacent to Fire Station, Manchester Road
1914	Electric tram service extended to Marsden
1923	Shakespeare Inn on Peel Street, replacing an older inn built nearby but lower down
1925	The Old Ram Inn closed
1928	Church School, The Old Ram, Hall etc demolished
c1935	Woods Council Estate off Meltham Road
1944	Canal closed to traffic
c1950	Dirker Council Estate above Marsden Lane
1957	Netherley Council Estate off Mount Road

1960s	Buildings on western side of Towngate demolished and old churchyard laid out as gardens
1960s	Wessen Court, Towngate
1967	National School demolished
1974	Houses on river side of Argyle Street demolished
2001	Canal reopened

Extensive private housing estates above Carrs Road and Clough Lea, etc and ribbon development along Stubbin Road, Meltham Road, Waters Road and Marsden Lane

Sources

Written materials

Bygone Marsden   Lawrence B. Whitehead 1942. Percy Brothers Ltd

The Black Flood   G. Brown 1987 In The Saddleworth Historical Society Bulletin vol. 17 no. 3

Colne Valley Cloth   Phyllis Bentley 1946 Huddersfield & District Woollen Export Group Republished as *The Pennine Weaver* 1971 by Firecrest

The Construction of the Huddersfield Narrow Canal 1794 - 1811   R.B. Schofield 1992 in *Huddersfield: A Most Handsome Town* ed. E. A. Hilary Haigh Kirklees Cultural Services

The History of the Colne Valley   D.F. E. Sykes 1906. Published in 10 parts by F. Walker. Republished in facsimile 1988 by Tollhouse Books

The History of Marsden Congregational Church   Rev. Luke Beaumont 1900. G. W. Owen

Huddersfield Highways Down the Ages   W. B. Crump 1949. Tolson Memorial Museum

Huddersfield Narrow Canal   K. Gibson & D. Finnis 2010. The Horizon Press

The Leeds Huddersfield and Manchester Railway written and published by Martin Bairstow 1984. Revised and enlarged 1990

The Life & Times of John Metcalf, commonly known as Blind Jack of Knaresborough   Anon 1795. Old Hall Press 1989

Marsden Children: Their Work in the Mills and the History of their Education   Judi Thorpe 2011. Marsden History Group

Marsden Memories   Marsden Festival Committee 1979

Marsden Milennium Memoirs   Marsden Enhancement and Residents' Society 2000.

Marsden Through the Ages   E. Irene Pearson 1984.

Marsden Park Centenary 1912 - 2012   2012. Friends of Marsden Park.

Marsden - Then and Now: A Photographic Journey   Marsden History Group 2008.

Pennine Passage   M & P Fox 1989. Huddersfield Canal Society.

Prehistoric People of the Pennines   P. A. Spikins 2002. West Yorkshire Archaeological Service

The Romans Came this Way   N. Lunn et. al. 2008. Huddersfield and District Archaeological Society

Standedge Guide   G. Keevil 1986. Kirklees Metropolitan Council

Saint Bartholomew's Church, Marsden 1453 - 1980   E. Irene Pearson 1981.

William Schofield, an Earnest Yorkshire Methodist   John Sykes 1882. Parkin Bros.

Marsden Manor   Peter Whitehead (unpublished)

Colne Valley Guardian back numbers   held by West Yorkshire Archive Service

Huddersfield Examiner back numbers   held by West Yorkshire Archive Service

Leeds Mercury back numbers   held by the British Library

Marsden Parish Burial Register

Saint Bartholomew's Church Parish Magazines

Maps used

John Warburton 1720, scale 1 inch to 2½ miles

A new & correct map of the County of York in all it's divisions: by actual survey and dimensuration: with the arms and seats of the nobility and gentry...

The map was largely the result of Warburton's tours of the county in 1718 and 1719. He seems to have been more interested in heraldry and Roman antiquities than in topography, but the map is significant in that it is the first to depict Yorkshire at such a large scale. It is poorly surveyed, and of little interest in the context of Marsden's history. It merely marks the position of Marsden Chapel (the old church), with the unnamed Colne following an entirely fanciful course. The Roman road is marked as a pair of ruled lines running diagonally across the map, regardless of any topographical obstacles.

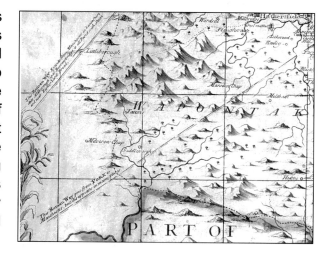

The copy we used is in the Harold Whittaker Collection, University of Leeds, and is reproduced with the permission of Leeds University Library, Special Collections.

Thomas Jefferys 1771-2, scale 1" to 1 mile

The County of York. survey'd in MDCCLLXVII. VIII. IX AND MCCCLXX

The first accurately surveyed map of Yorkshire, this is a landmark document. A major aim of the publisher was to map the main roads in the county. It gives us our first glimpse of the size and shape of the village, with many individual buildings marked, and many of these named. Some of the un-named buildings do, however, appear to be placed rather randomly Our copy of the map was kindly provided by Alan Petford from his original.

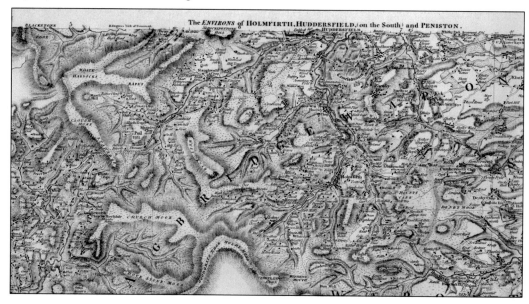

Map of the route of the Huddersfield Canal: 1793 scale not known

This map was made by Nicholas Brown before the canal was constructed, to show the ownership of the land through which the canal would go.

As a result, it maps Marsden-in-Huddersfield in reasonable detail.

Reference. 150361 QDP 6 Cheshire Archives and Local Studies (CALS)

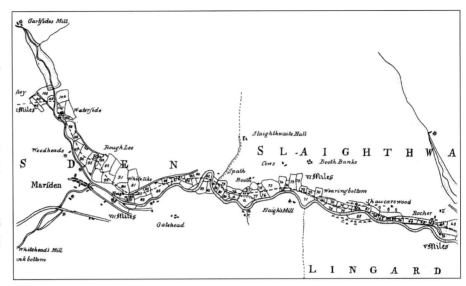

Plan of the Canal between Huddersfield in the County of York and Ashton Under Lyne in the County of Lancaster B[enjamin] Outram, engineer, and N Brown, surveyor.1794. No scale given

National Waterways Archive BW128-213

This excellent map helps to fill in some of the gaps between Jefferys' and Greenwood's maps. Although made to show the route of the then proposed canal, it maps Marsden in some detail and from a much more accurate survey than either of them. We are grateful to the Waterways Archive/ Canal and River Trust for permission to publish it.

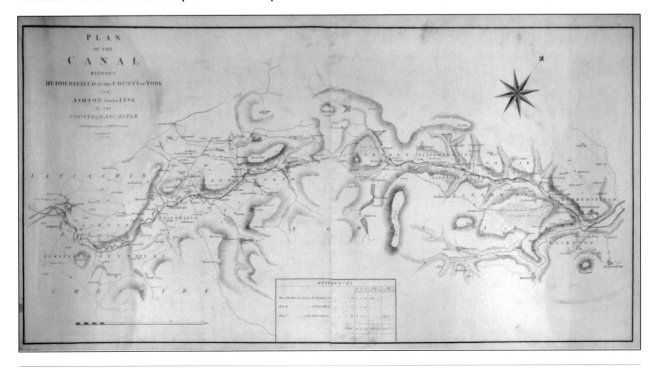

Marsden-in-Almondbury Township Map 1801 presumed surveyed by John Johnson 1799/1800. West Yorkshire Archive Service, Kirklees. Re. KC 500. scale not known.

The first detailed survey of the township. One of its functions was to map the then ownership of the land in copyhold. Together with its associated record book, it also gives all the field names with their acreages.

The original map is very large (c. 3.3 x 2 metres) and in a very poor state. Huddersfield Library archive section holds a copy in the form of 35 A3 photographed sections. Some parts are very rubbed and/or faint, and the photographed sheets do not join neatly. Keith Hemsley has spliced together the sections we used.

We are grateful to West Yorkshire Archive Service for permission to reproduce this map.

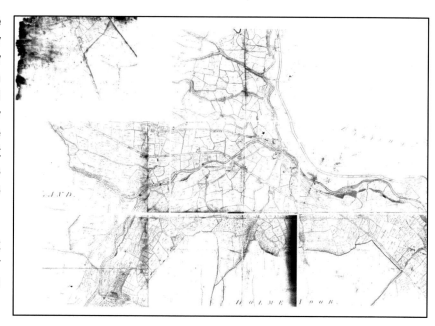

Marsden-in-Huddersfield Township Map 1801 presumed surveyed 1799/1800, scale not known

The copy we have of this map does not cover the whole of Marsden-in-Huddersfield, missing everything west of Tunnel End Reservoir. It served the same functions as the map for Marsden-in-Almondbury.

We have made every endeavour to find the original of this map without success. If any reader has any information, please let us know.

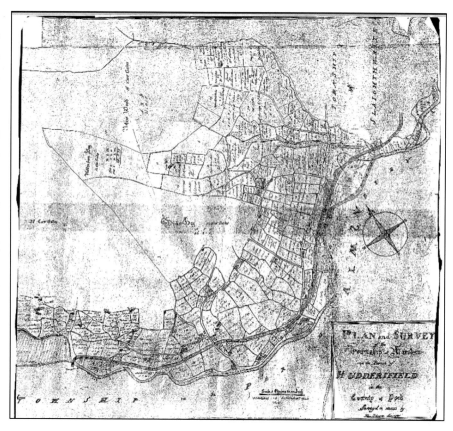

Christopher Greenwood 1818 surveyed 1815-17, scale 3/4" to 1 mile

Map of the county of York: made on the basis of triangles in the county determined by Lieu. Col. W. Mudge.

Greenwood was able to take advantage of the Ordnance Survey's Triangulation of England as a basis for his map, giving it more accuracy than Jefferys'. The map is important because of this, and because it shows significant changes which had occurred in Marsden during the forty years since Jefferys' map.

The copy we used is in the Harold Whittaker Collection, University of Leeds, and is reproduced with the permission of Leeds University Library, Special Collections.

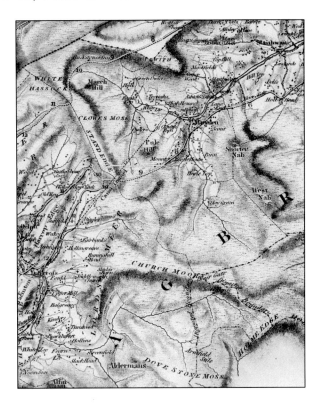

Marsden-in-Almondbury Tithe Map 1848 presumed surveyed 1846-1847, scale not known.

The map is drawn with north on the right. National Archive reference no. IR 30/43/276

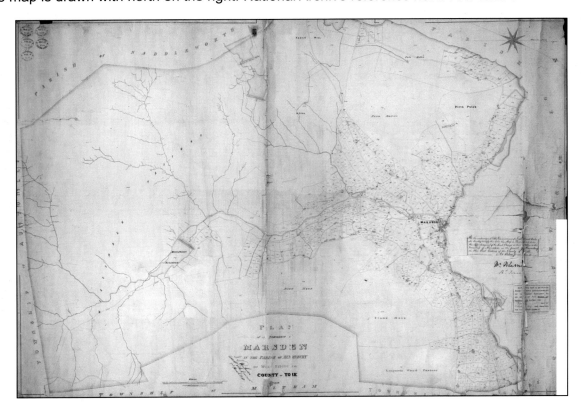

Marsden in Huddersfield Tithe Map 1850 presumed surveyed 1846 - 1847, scale not known. The map is drawn with north on the left. National Archive reference no. IR 30/43/277

Tithes were established in pre-Conquest times and were annual payments made to the Church by residents of every parish. After the reformation they were paid to the Church of England regardless of the

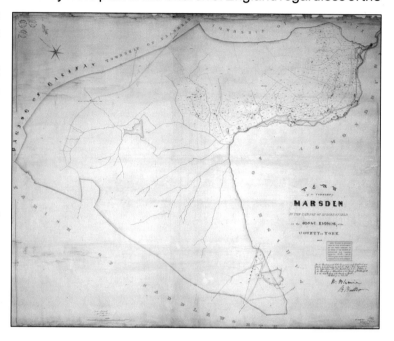

religious affiliation of the payer. Tithes were originally paid in kind but there was a gradual movement towards cash payments. The Tithe Commutation Act of 1836 was a significant part of this process, causing land to be assessed in order to establish a cash payment. This required the making of accurate maps of each parish to establish land ownership and acreage.

These maps were intended to be of the highest quality. Those for Marsden are very accurate, and compare very well to the first Ordnance Survey map published only a few years later. The copies we used are held at the National Archive at Kew. We are grateful to the National Archive for permission to reproduce these maps.

1st, Edition, 6" to 1 mile Ordnance Survey Map of Yorkshire (West Riding) 1854. Surveyed 1849 - 1851

This beautiful map gives a wealth of accurate detail about Marsden in the mid-19th century, at a time just after the Leeds to Manchester railway was built through the Colne Valley.

The original map is composed of many rectangular sheets pasted onto a linen backing, with a gap of about 5mm between each of them. Saddleworth Historical Society kindly scanned the relevant section of their copy for Marsden History Group, and Nick Pollett then spent many hours on the computer to remove the gaps between the individual sheets.

Map of central Marsden c1870. West Yorkshire Archive Service, Kirklees. Ref. KC391/85. Scale not known

This very valuable map forms part of the documentation for a sale, found in the John Marsden papers in the archives in Huddersfield Central Library.

The Mechanics' Institute is shown, which opened in 1861, as is the original Snail Horn Bridge, which was rebuilt in 1891.

We are grateful to West Yorkshire Archive Service for permission to reproduce this map.

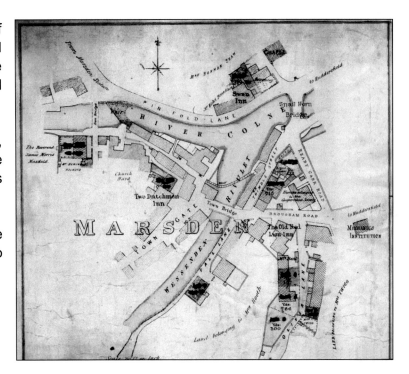

1904 Ordnance Survey 25" to 1 mile map of Marsden.

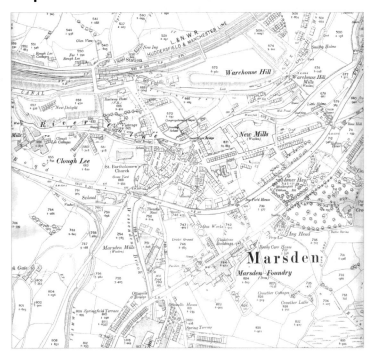

The following 6" to 1 mile maps have been used, and are located in Marsden Library, where they are available for inspection.
1895 Ordnance Survey sheet CCLIX N.E. resurveyed and revised 1890
1908 Ordnance Survey sheet CCLIX N.E.survey revised 1904
1949 Ordnance Survey sheet CCLIX S.E revision of 1938